THE ALLEGHENY PILOT

T0339925

METALMARK BOOKS

THE

ALLEGHENY PILOT;

CONTAINING A COMPLETE CHART OF THE

ALLEGHENY RIVER,

SHOWING THE ISLANDS AND BARS AND

LOW WATER CHANNEL

FROM

WARREN TO PITTSBURGH,

ALSO

A TABLE OF DISTANCES FOR ALL THE PRINCIPAL WESTERN NAVIGABLE
RIVERS.

BY E. L. BABBITT, Photo.

E. L. BABBITT, PUBLISHER AND PRINTER;
FREEPORT, PA.
. . . .
1855.

IF YOU ARE TROUBLED WITH LIVER COMPLAINT,

OR ANY DISEASE ARISING FROM EXCESS OF BILE ON THE STOMACH,

USE DR. M'LANE'S

CELEBRATED LIVER PILLS.

PREPARED BY

FLEMING BROS. Sole Proprietors.

THE INCREASED DEMAND FOR DR. M'LANE'S LIVER PILLS.

Since their introduction, has far exceeded the most sanguine expectations of the Proprietors. It is now eighteen years since they were first brought before the public, during which time *thousands of certificates*, from persons of respectability, who have used *Dr. M'Lane's Pills with the most happy results*, have been handed us.

We have also the certificates of a large number of *Regular Physicians*, of good standing, throughout the country, who are using and recommending these Pills in their practice.

Dr M'Lane's Liver Pills are not, like most of the popular medicines of the day, held forth or recommended as universal cure-alls, but simply for

LIVER COMPLAINTS,

Or diseases originating in a deranged state of that organ. We have lately received letters from many who have used these Pills in

CASES OF AGUE AND FEVER,

With the most happy results. Certainly no better cathartic can be used preparatory to or after taking quinine. We would advise all who are afflicted with this disease to give them a fair trial. In case of

BILLIOUS FEVER, AND INDEED ALL BILIOUS COMPLAINTS,

We unhesitatingly pronounce Dr. M'Lane's Liver Pills to be one of the most safe and effectual remedies now before the public.

Symptoms of a Diseased Liver,

Pain in the right side, under the edge of the ribs, increasing on pressure; sometimes the pain is in the left side; the patient is rarely able to lie on the left side; sometimes the pain is felt under the Shoulder blade, and it frequently extends to the top of the shoulder, and is sometimes mistaken for a rheumatism in the arm. The stomach is affected with loss of appetite and sickness; the bowels in general are costive, sometimes alternating with lax: the head is troubled with pain, accompanied with a dull, heavy sensation in the back part. There is generally a considerable loss of memory, accompanied with a painful sensation of having left undone something which ought to have been done. A slight dry cough is sometimes an attendant. The patient complains of weariness and debility; he is easily startled; his feet are cold or burning, and he complains of a prickly sensation of the skin; his spirits are low, and although he is satisfied that exercise would be beneficial to him, yet he can scarcely summon up fortitude enough to try it. In fact, he distrusts every remedy. Several of the above symptoms attend the disease; but cases have occurred where few of them existed, yet examination of the body, after death, has shown the Liver to have been extensively deranged.

☞Purchasers will be careful to ask for Dr. M'Lane's celebrated Liver Pills, manufactured by Fleming Bros. of Pittsburgh, Pa. All other Vermifuges in comparison are worthless, Dr. M'Lane's genuine Liver Pills, also his celebrated Vermifuge, can now be had at all respectable drug stores. None genuine without the signature of

FLEMING BROS. Druggists,

No. 60 Wood St. Pittsburgh, Pa. U. S. A. Sole Proprietors.

THE
ALLEGHENY PILOT;

CONTAINING A COMPLETE CHART OF THE ALLEGHENY RIVER
SHOWING THE ISLANDS AND BARS, AND LOW WATER
CHANNEL, FROM WARREN TO PITTSBURGH,
WITH DIRECTIONS FOR NAVIGA-
TING THE SAME WITH

RAFTS, FLAT-BOATS, ETC:

AND

INTENDED FOR THE BENEFIT OF RIVERMEN GENERALLY.

ALSO
A VARIETY OF HISTORICAL
MATTER, CONTAINING REMINISCENCES OF PLACES
ALONG THE RIVER, AND MANY INCIDENTS WHICH TRANSPIRED
IN THE EARLY HISTORY OF THE COUNTRY, BOTH CIVIL AND MILITARY, AND
AN ABRIDGED HISTORY OF THE ABORIGINESE OF THE COUNTRY THROUGH WHICH THE
RIVER PASSES, WITH BIOGRAPHICAL SKETCHES, INTERESTING TO ALL CON-
CERNED IN THE NAVIGATION OF THIS BEAUTIFUL RIVER

ALSO

A TABLE OF DISTANCES FOR ALL THE PRINCIPAL WESTERN NAVIGABLE RIVERS.

BY E. L. BABBITT, Photo.

E. L. BABBITT, PUBLISHER AND PRINTER;
FREEPORT, PA.
. . . .
1855.

Price one Dollar.

PREFACE.

In presenting this work to the public, the author begs leave to say that he believes the river to be so completely pictured—the Islands, bars, and channels so minutely described in the directions, and the distances from place to place so correctly given, that the "wayfaring man, though a fool, need not err therein."

It is believed by the intelligent portion of the community where this book will be most useful, that a work of the kind here presented, has been greatly needed for many years past. The author not only hopes to enable those who may see fit to engage in the navigation of the river, to do it with safty, precission and confidence, but to enliven in their minds a spirit of inquiry into the history of their own immediate neighborhoods.

The work is intended principally for those who decend the river with rafts of lumber, flat-boats, etc. Those who are desirous of becoming thoroughly acquainted with the river for the purpose of learning to pilot, will find it greatly to their interest to thoroughly examine its pages, which will readily associate the memory with the most important and difficult places to navigate, and also to familiarize the mind with the names of Islands, Bars, Creeks, Runs, Eddies, etc., with their relative distances. Many times it is worth the price of the book to even be told of a good Eddy to land in. Those who are studying the river as a professsion, for the purpose of becoming Steamboat Pilots, will derive much benefit from a thorough knowledge of this work, which would enable them to answer many questions, during their inspection, relative to the names of places, Islands-bars, low water channel, distances, etc., which must otherwise require several years time and experience to become acquainted with. Having had no experience in the management of Steamboats, we forego giving directions on that point.

For many of the historical and biographical sketches contained in this work we are indebted to Craig's History of Pittsburgh, Col. Stone's Life of Red Jacket, and Day's Historical Collections of Pennsylvania. We have not only had recourse to the above works, but have spent much time in conversing with many of the oldest settlers along the river, collecting from them, orally, many historical facts besides those pertaining to the navigation of the river.

THE ALLEGHENY RIVER.

Probably no river in the world, rolls for the same distance, such a clear and pure current; hence it received its name, "Allegheny," from the Seneca Indians, meaning "Fair Water." For the same cause, it was called by the French, "La Belle Rivere." It rises in the northern part of Pennslvania, passes through a small portion of New York, and winding its way back into Pennsylvania again, runs with its meanderings, not less than fifty miles within the county of Warren. It also flows through the centre of Venango county, in a direction so very curvical, that there is not a point of the compass to which it does not direct its course. The country along its banks is exceedingly wild and rugged; the river hills being high and precipitous, rising into bluffs and cliffs, sometimes to the height of 300 feet. These bluffs exhibit a wild and picturesque grandeur, well calculated to call forth from the reflecting lover of nature, "Oh! Lord how stupenduous are thy Works." The country on the head waters of the Allegheny yet contains almost inexhaustible supplies of first rate pine lumber· It is supposed that from thirty to fifty million feet of plank and boards, and from fifty to seventy million shingles, decend the river annually. Further down, the hills are rich with Iron ore of an excellent quality, and Bituminous coal, by which Iron is manufactured in immense quantities. There is not hardly a point on the river, below Franklin, that the sound of the steam whistle of the furnace engine, cannot be heard.

The country along the Allegheny, from Warren to Pittsbnrgh, is now inhabited by an intelligent, indurtrious, hospitable, and friendly people. Roll back a century! What a contrast!! Instead of the present enlightened people, this whole region was occupied by the Seneca Indians. The untutored Indian and his rude wigwam is substituted for the sacred Preacher and house of God; the scalp yell for the steam whistle; the bark canoe for the steamboat. Traces are to be found, in almost every direction, of a numerous Indian population once inhabiting this region; and a more appropriate one could hardly be found for their residence. The rugged hills clothed with forest, and abounding with game—the pure sparkling streams flowing among the hills, furnished them excellent fishing grounds, bordered here and there with bottom land, as sites for their villages and cornfields. The Senecas, of which Cornplanter was Chief, was far the most numerous and warlike of the Six Nations. The peculiar organization of that confederacy, and the rank which the Senecas held in it, were as follows: This confederacy was originally known in the annals of New York as the Five Nations; and subsequently, being joined by the Tuscaroras, as the Six Nations. As confederates, they called themselves *Aquanuschroni*, or "United People." They were called by the French, Iroquois. The original Five Nations were the Onondagas, the Cayugas, the Oneidas, the Senecas, and the Mohawks. In 1712 the Tuscaroras being expelled from the interior of North Carolina and Virginia, were adopted as the sixth tribe. The language of all the tribes of the confederacy, except the Tuscaroras was radically the same. Their domain stretched from the borders of Vermont to Lake Erie and from Lake Ontario to the head waters of the Allegheny Susquehanna and Delaware rivers. This Teritory they styled their *Long House*. The Grand council fire was held in the Onondaga valley. The Senecas guarded the western door of the house, the Mohawks the eastern, and the Cayugas the southern or that which opened upon the Susquehanna. The Mohawk nation was the first in rank, and to it appertained the office of principal war chief. To the Onondagas, who guarded the council-fire, appertained in like manner the office of principal civil chief or sachem. The Senecas in numbers and military energy were the most powerful. The peculiar location of the Iroquois on the great channels of water conveyence to which their territories were contiguous, gave them a great advantage. And by an early alliance with the Dutch on the Hudson, they secured the use of firearms, and were thus enabled not only to repel the encroachment of the French, but in all directions to carry war and devastation, and reduce to a state of vasselage many Indian nations. But on them, like everything else, is written, "Passing away." If the future whispers what the prst will justify us in believing, the general bury ground of their whole race is at no very remote period. The history of their wrongs at the hands of land speculators would fill a larger book than this. By various treaties they have been deprived of one piece of their fair domain after another, until this once powerful nation are now crowded upon four small reservations, one at Tonawanda eight miles N. W. of Batavia, one three miles east of Buffalo, one at Cattaraugus Creek twenty-eight miles south of Buffalo, and the fourth on the Allegheny seventeen miles above Warren. This reservation was the late residence of Cornplanter, the distinguished Seneca chief. At each of these reservations except Tonawanda, the American Board have a Mission station with a Church and schools.

THE
ALLEGHENY PILOT.

---o---

WARREN:

---o---

WARREN, the county seat of Warren County, is situated on the right. It is principally built along the river bank, which is about 35 feet above the water. It is allowed to be one of the most elligible sites on the river; and commands a picturesque view above and below. It was incorporated a Borough in 1832. Near the centre of the plat, and about one-fourth of a mile from the river, is the Public Square, or *Diamond;* around which are situated the public buildings. The Court House and Academy, are built of brick; and the Jail, Prothonotary's Office, and the building formerly occupied by the *Lumberman's Bank,* are of stone. The Prothonotary's Office, which is situated near the Court House, was burned in December, 1854. The building contained the usual offices of the county, with the public documents, which were all saved, except those of the Commissioners' Office where the fire was supposed to have originated. The walls, through the vigilance of the Fire Company, assisted by the citizens, suffered no material injury. It was enlarged and rebuilt in the following year. The place contains five churches; the Methodis Episcopal, German Methodist, Presbyterian, Lutheran, and Roman Catholic. The dwellings and stores are generally of wood, well built and neatly painted. There are also a number of costly and magnificent brick buildings which have been erected within a few years past, among which are the Carver House, Tanner, Watson, and Johnson Blocks.

The settlement of Warren County was greatly retarded by the misconstructions and litigations resulting from the Land Law of 1792, and the peculiar management of the Holland Land Company. who by way of aiding and encouraging settlers upon their lands, established a large storehouse at Warren, one of the first buildings in the place. The Pine Lumbering business being the great object of pursuit among the settlers; and not agriculture, (and so long as they had but the color of a title,) they would remain long enough upon the land to cut all the valuable timber, and then take "French leave," squat upon a new tract, and set up a claim to that. This state of affairs brought many of the settlers and the Company's Agents into continual conflicts and litigations. The latter refused to sell to such persons any thing from their store, or in any way to countenance them, without a compromise with the company. During this state of uncertainties, the better class of people were detered from purchas ing, and the population in 1810, was only 827; and in 1820 was less than 2000. Warren, in common with the county, was retarded in its improvements by the same causes; and in 1813 it could boast of but five houses. In 1850 its population was 1010, it is now, probably, 1500. The seat of justice was fixed at Warren at the organization of the county, on the 16th of March, 1819. It is 120 miles from Pittsburgh, by land, and 203 by the river. The business of Warren varies with the seasons of the year. During the rafting freshes, the whole country round about, as well as Warren, presents a business like appearance; all is alive with the bustle of preparation among the lumbermen. Rafts of smaller dimentions, from the upper Allegheny and Conewango Creek, with their numerous and busy population, are continually pouring into the eddy to be coupled into those of larger area, or what is called Pittsburgh Fleets; in which shape they pursue their journey to Pittsburgh and Cincinnati. Indeed, it is a sort of harvest, and General Jail Delivery, to almost every kind of business. The Tavern-keepers, Merchants, and Mechanics, all reap their peculiar benefits at these seasons. Steamboats are frequently seen winding their way up the river, puffing and snorting around the circuitous bends, discharging their cargoes of merchandise, produce, etc., at the wharves, then wheeling about and plying steam, are soon out of sight on their way back to the Iron City.

Warren may be considered at the head of steam navigation on the Allegheny river, in consequence of mill dams having been built above, which obstruct the passage of steamboats altogether, which can only get this far in times of high water. Heavy freighted Keelboats from Pittsburgh also arrive here, and depart, at almost every season of the year. The Eddy is sufficiently large and commodious, so that a number of Pittsburgh fleets can be coupled in it at the same time. Rafts can be landed on both sides of the river, any where above the bridge; but the right is by far the most prferable, especially in very high water. Flat boats can be wintered her in perfect safty; and also rafts, by uncoupling and drawing them up past the wharf toward the mills, but they are not safe if left anywhere in the eddy below; for, if not entirely destroyed, they are liable to suffer more or less injury when the ice breaks up.

The splendid bridge that once crossed the Allegheny, is now gone. A portion of it was unroofed in a gale of wind, and was never repaired. In this condition, it remained exposed to the rain and storms for about ten years, when the portion most injured and exposed, became so rotten that it gave way and fell with a tremendous crash. The remaining part fell about a year after. The mason work yet remains. The elegant stone pier on which the centre of the superstructure rested, stands in the middle of the river, and at the lower end of the eddy, a perfect monument of neglect.

DIRECTIONS FOR MAP NO. 1.

MORRISON'S BARS. - - - - - - - - - | 1 | 1

After passing the pier, keep nearest the right shore down to the head of the riffle, which is nearly one-half mile above the bars, and when about half way down the riffle, incline over nearly to the middle, in order to pass between the two bars— one on the right, the other on the left, and a few rods below. In high water little or no notice need be taken of the one on the right.

REESE'S EDDY, on the right. - - - - - - | 1¾ | 2¾

From Morrison's bars keep near the middle till around the bend, then incline to the left to pass the bars a few rods above the eddy. These bars are of no account in high water.

MEAD'S ISLAND. - - - - - - - - - - - | ½ | 3¼

This Island is by far the largest and most valuable of any on the river below Warren. It is about one mile in length, contains about 300 acres, and is valued at $7,000. The Island is owned by a Mrs. Mead, a widow lady.

Channel to the right or left; but the right side is most feasible, as it will save crossing back to the right again above the Grass Flat Islands.

Mead's bar makes out from the Island about one-fourth of a mile below the head. It reaches nearly half way from the Island to the right shore, and throws a strong current into the right bank. In low running stages the channel has a rather short turn around the end of the bar, as will be seen by the chart. When past the foot of the Island, keep near the right shore to prepare for

JACKSON'S and GRASS FLAT ISLANDS. - - - | 1¼ | 4¼

These Islands have hitherto proved themselves rather troublesome customers to many of the lumbermen. But, to assign a reasonable cause for many of the thousand dollars worth of lumber being torn in pieces upon them, would be a task that *some* of the parties concerned would rather be excused from undertaking. Sometimes pilots from some cause, or no cause at all, have undertaken to go to the left of Jackson's Island, and by so doing, have frequently got into hot water

WARREN

Bridge

Morrison's Bars

ALLEGHENY Nº 1.

Reese's Eddy

Reese's Bars

Sills

Mead's Isl.

Mead's Bar

Sill's Run

D. Jackson's

E. Robertson's
R. Leonard's
J. Hodges

Jackson's Isl.

Grass Flat Isl.

Lower Grass Flat Isl.

East

North

Scot's Run

Woods

Scot's Isl.

Scot's Eddy

Brokenstraw Isl.

Brokenstraw Race

Brokenstraw Eddy

Irvin's Run

Wm A. Irvin's H.

Wm Schuchman & Bro. Lith. Pittsb.

themselves, and in some instances brought others in with them. There is no need of ever going to the left of this Island with a raft. The deepest, safest, and best channel, is to the extreme right of all these Islands, till past the lower Grass Flat. And when down even with the foot of the last named Island, hold to the left, and prepare for

SCOTT'S ISLAND. - - - - - - - - - - -   1¼   6

Channel to the left. This Island is a kind of a Tadpole shaped thing, lying close to the right shore. There is but little water to the right of it. At the foot of the Island, on the right, is Scott's Eddy.

BIG BROKENSTRAW CREEK. - - - - - -   1   7

This creek rises in Erie County, Pa., and after receiving the waters of Coffee, Hair, Spring, Mullengar, and the Little Brokenstraw Creeks, empties into the Allegheny about seven miles below Warren. The Little Brokenstraw takes its rise in Chautauque County, not far from the head waters of French Creek, and empties into the Big Brokenstraw 7 miles above its mouth. The lumbering business is extensively pursued on all the above named tributaries. From four to six million feet of lumber, and from ten to fifteen million shingles, go down the Allegheny from this point every year. A few rods below the mouth of the creek, on the right, is Brokenstraw Eddy, the great place of preparation for all the Brokenstraw lumbermen. The village and land for a considerable distance around, is owned entirely by Dr. Wm. A. Irvine, grandson of Gen. Wm. Irvine of the Revolutionary army, who was for several years engaged as Commissioner for the State, in superintending the survey of lands north-west of the Allegheny under the land law of 1792.

Dr. Wm. A. Irvine inherited this land from his father, the late commissory Gen. Calendar Irvine, who came to this place in 1795, erected a cabin, and placed it in charge of a faithful negro servant, by way of perfecting an "actual settlement."

On the flats near the Eddy, once stood an Indian village, called *Buckaloon*, which was destroyed by a detachment under Col. Baoadhead, from Pittsburgh, in 1781. It required a siege of several days to drive out the Indians, who retreated to the hills in the rear of the village. Several days afterwards,

Maj. Morrison (afterwards a distinguished citizen of Lexing-
ton, Ky.,) returned to reconnoitre, and had stooped down to
drink at the mouth of the creek, when a ball from an Indian's
rifle splashed the water in his face. This fact was long after
confirmed to Dr. Irvine, by one of Cornplanters men.

The traveler in passing through this vicinity, will notice a
neat little stone Church, situated in a beautiful grove, and
also a stone School House on the opposite side of the road,
These, we are told, were erected at the expense of Mrs. Dr.
Wm. A. Irvine, who possessed an ample fortune of her own.

One can easily form some idea of the taste and refinement
of this amiable lady, when we view the scenery around this
place, for she has chosen one of Nature's most inviting re-
treats, and one every way calculated to draw the thinking
mind from nature up to nature's God.

She was a worthy member of the Presbyterian Church,
and although she never talked so loudly of Woman's Rights,
as a Mrs. Bloomer, or claimed a right to minister in holy
things, as does the *Rev.* Antionette Brown, still, her life
was useful, her Christian zeal and consistent piety was
evinced by deeds of benevolence and charity.

But human life is short. Decay, change and death,
have fixed their seals upon the face of all nature; and all on
earth we cherish and cling to most fondly, is forced from our
embrace, leaving the sorrowful heart to brood over the urn of
hallowed memory. In the midst of her labors, she went to
her reward. Her funeral sermon was the first one preached
in the house. Her mortal remains slumber in the pleasant
grove that surrounds the church; but the memory of her many
virtues will be cherished by coming generations, and perhaps
encourage others of her sex to generous and noble deeds.

BROKENSTRAW ISLAND. - - - - - - - -   4¾   7¾

Channel to the right. This Island is owned by Dr. Wm. A·
Irvine. It is about three fourths of a mile long, and contains
63 acres of cultivated land.

From the head of the Island in low water, keep near the
middle, and when nearly down to Dr. Irvine's house, incline
to the right to avoid the bar on the left about oposite the
house, when past the bar, keep a little to the right of the
middle till down to the foot of the Island,

Rafts can, and do, sometimes, go to the left, but it should
not be done unless by accident they are driven on the left
shore above. The water is about eight inches deeper to the
right.

DIRECTIONS FOR MAP NO. 2.

J. THOMPSONS ISLAND. - - - - - - - - | 2 | 9¾

This Island is owned by Mr. James Thompson, it is over a mile long and contains 57 acres of cultivated land.

Channel to the right. In low water keep very near the right shore, around the right point below Dunn's Eddy, and till around to the mountain which will carry you clear of the large bars that make out from the head of the Island, and keep also near the right shore till past Deerfield bar which is bleow the middle of the Island and reaches about half way from the Island to the right shore.

Rafts that are coupled on the left above the Island, usualy go to the left, but in such cases they have to cross immediately to the right at the foot in order to run to the right of Clarks Island. Deerfield Bar derives its name from Deerfield township line which crosses it, it should be well looked to in all stages of water.

After passing the foot of the Island keep near the right shore down to

CLARK'S ISLAND. - - - - - - - - - - | 1¾ | 11½

Chanel to the right. Enter the chute about midway between the Island and right shore, then incline a little to the right to avoid a bar that makes out from the Island a little below the head, and from this point keep near the right shore till down to the foot. There is no channel to the left, it is cut to pieces by willow bars at the foot of the Island.

ROBERT THOMPSON'S ISLAND. - - - - - | 1¼ | 12¾

Channel to the right or left, but the main trvel is to the right in all stages of water, although the greatest portion of the river runs to the left. From the foot of Clark's Island keep near the right shore so as to be within a few feet of it while passing the head of the Island. This will carry you clear of the large flat bar which makes out from the head of the Island and reaches over half way to the right shore, when past the bar run over to the left about half way to the Island.

In passing along from the foot of Clark's Island don't be deceived by the strong current that makes to the left, rafts have thus been drawn over far enough to have easily went to the left of the Island, and when too late have tried to get back, and by so doing run upon the bar spoken of.

In going to the left of the Island observe a large rock about three rods from the left shore and a little above the foot of the Island, and also a little middle bar immediately below the foot.

STEWARD ISLANDS. - ` - - - - ` - -	1¾	14½

The first of these Islands contains 15 acres and is owned by Mrs. Magee, a widow lady. The other, 20 acres and belongs to Peter Smith.

Channel to the right. In fair running stages when down to the foot of the first Island or where the channel comes in between the Islands, begin to make your crossing in order to go to the left of Charley Smith's Bars, Mill Stone Island etc. This is the first general crossing place below Warren.

CHARLEY SMITH'S BARS. - - - - - -	1½	16

The ice gorge in 1853 nearly ruined this portion of the river for running rafts in low water. There are no less than four different channels and neither of them sufficiently deep, wide and straight to run large rafts through with safty. The usual and best of these in a fair running stage is the left shore channel over bar No. 2; this bar having been formed by the ice, extends across the channel in the form of what is known by the rivermen as a "pocket" or "fish basket" and is the one on which rafts are frequently stopped in low running.

The second, in order to designate, we call the left centre channel, is made by bar No. 2, in turning the main current abruptly to the right between it and bar No, 1. This channel is the deepest of the four by nearly a foot; but so crooked that a large raft cannot turn in it.

The third in order we call the right centre channel, is between the tow head and bar No. 1, and is bout two inches deeper than the left channel on bar No. 2.

The fourth is to the right of the tow heads. While pass-

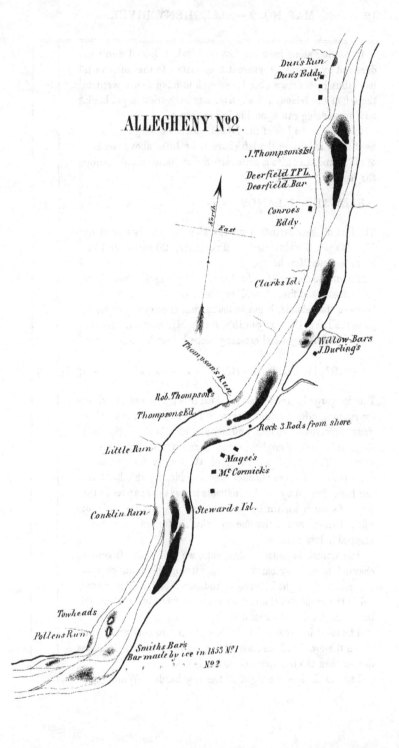

ALLEGHENY Nº2.

Dun's Run
Dun's Eddy

J. Thompson's Isl.

Deerfield T.P.L.
Deerfield Bar

Conroe's
Eddy

North   East

Clarks Isl.

Willow Bars
J. Durling's

Thompson's Run

Rob. Thompson's

Thompsons Ed.

Rock 3 Rods from shore

Little Run

Magee's
McCormick's

Conklin Run   Steward's Isl.

Towheads

Pollens Run

Smiths Bars
Bar made by ice in 1853 Nº 1
Nº 2

ing the bar that extends from the tow heads diagonally up wards, keep very near the right shore. The greatest objection to this channel, is its being narrow and crooked; although some think it the best in low water, it being several inches deeper than either of the others, except the left centre.

DIRECTIONS FOR MAP NO. 3.

MILL STONE ISLAND. - ، ، - - ، - . - -	1	17

Channel to the left, about the center of the left chute. Those who live in the immediate vicinity of these Islands do on some occasions go to the right, and in some instances run between the two, but it requires close calculations besides being left on the rong side of the river below. In going to the right the channel is quite near the head of the Isalnd in consequence of a bar which makes out from the right shore.

GOOSE FALT ISLAND. - - - - ، - ، -	1	18

Channel to the left. There is also a channel to the right, but it is not traveled much except by those who couple timber rafts at the mouth of Magee's run.

MAGEE'S BAR. - - - - - - ، - - - ، ،	1	19

Channel to the right. After leaving the lower Goose Flat Island keep near the middle; and while passing the bar be a little nearest the right shore then incline over to the left.

COURSON ISLANDS. ، - - ، - - - - -	¾	19¾

Channel to the left. There is no navigable channel to the right in consequence of a mill dam which crosses it.

MAGUYER'S BAR. - - - - - - - - - -	1¼	21

Channel to the right. This bar is situated on the left a few rods above the foot of the third and last Coursn Island. It reaches from the left shore about half way to the Island; in passing it in low water get two-thirds of the river to the left.

TIDIOUTE is situated on the right side, It comprises two considerable villages—Upper and Lower Tidioute, which are about a mile apart. It contains a number of Stores, Taverns, Mechanic shops, etc., requisite for such a place. It contains also a Presbyterian and Methodist church. The Methodists erected a splendid new church the past year.

For real business, this place excells; although the traveler in passing through it in some seasons of the year, might, perhaps, think otherwise. It presents the liveliest aspect during the rafting freshes, there being no less than eight steam saw mills within a short distance; the greater portion of the lumber of which is drawn to this place and rafted. Some of the mills are furnished with temporary railroads on which the lumber is brought to the river, and some brought with teams.

The lumbering business in the neighborhood of Tidioute, furnishes employment for several hundred men, who do their trading principally here, and also board here during the rafting seasons, which gives the place a business-like appearance.

TIDIOUTE ISLAND. - - - - - - - - - .   1   22

In order to have a correct knowledge of this plase it is best to thoroughly examine the Chart. In high, or ordinary low running stage, rafts that come from above the Courson Islands always go to the left, but the center or channel which runs between the head of the Island and upper middle bar, crosses the boat channel, and runs to the right of the lower middle bar, is preferable in low water, the water being a few inches deeper than to the left of the Island. The right or low water boat channel turns to the right at the upper end of the eddy, and above the upper middle bar passes through the eddy and down the riffle about three rods from the right shore, crosses the center channel and runs down close to the Island and to the left of the lower middle bar. This channel is deeper than either of the others but too crooked at the heads of the upper and lower middle bars for rafts to get into. The bar on the right below Gordon's run reaches over half way to the foot of the Island.

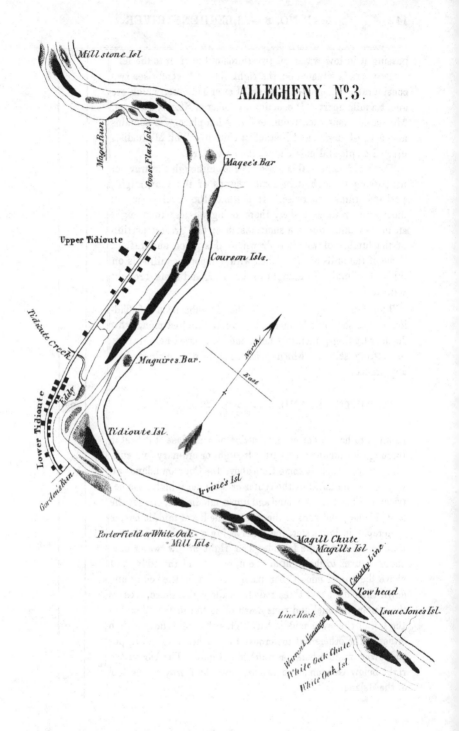

ALLEGHENY N°3.

Mill stone Isl.

Magee Run

Goose Flat Isls.

Magee's Bar

Upper Tidioute

Courson Isls.

Tidioute Creek

North

East

Maguires Bar.

Lower Tidioute

Eddy

Tidioute Isl.

Gordon's Run

Irvine's Isl

Porterfield or White Oak Mill Isls.

Magill Chute
Magill's Isl

County Line

Tow head

Line Rock

Isaac Jones's Isl.

Warrent Luanung

White Oak Chute

White Oak Isl.

Below the Island on the right is a very good eddy to land
rafts in. When past the Island cross to the right shore.

WHITE OAK ISLAND. - - - - - - - - -   4   26

From the foot of Tidioute Island to White Oak Island there
are no less than ten Islands and bars which gives the river a
ragged appearance. From the center to the left shore, it is
literaly cut to pieces with islands, bars and tow-heads; all of
which the channel is to the right. To discribe them minutely would be tedious as well as useless, besides they are well
defined in the chart, we will therefore animadvert to them col-
lectively and pass them by. In fair running stages there is
no feasible left hand channel between the above named points.
Magill's chute being filled up, and the channel at the foot of
Magill's Island is not safe in high water.

The far famed White oak chute which at present is the
main traveled path in high water, is to the right of the Island. This place in former years, was to the lumbermen,
what Thermopile was to the Persians, but latterly from its
beeing better understood little or no difficulty is experienced
in navigating it with the largest size rafts. Its principal pecu-
liaralities consists in its being narrow and crooked, besides
the swiftness of the water, the head bar of the Island being so
situated as to throw the current directly against the right
shore. The channel at the foot of Magill's Island is thought
by some to be better in low water than to the left of White
Oak Island, and is doubted by others, it certainly is not in
high water as there is much danger of being driven on the
bar below the Island.

The channel to the left of White Oak Island is considered
the best in low water and many like it the best in high water.
To run through this channel, hold over to the left, close to Isaac
Jone's Island after passing the little side bar near the head.

DIRECTIONS FOR MAP NO. 4.

HEMLOCK ISLANDS * - - - - - - - -   1¾   27¾

Channel to the left. In low water keep quite near the left
shore while passing the head bar of the Island, then incline
out nearly to the middle and when down near the foot of the

* These directions extend below Dorkaway Island and Siggin's Bar.

Island keep a little to the right of the middle till down to the foot of the third or lower Island, then steer a straight course down about the center of the river, between Prathers Bars passing to the right of Prather's Island, then incline to the left as you approach the bend below in order to avoid Siggin's bar which makes out from the right shore and reaches over half way across to Dorkaway Island, in very low water run quite near this Island.

The tow head that once stood on fishing bar about forty rods below the foot of the first of the Hemlock Islands, was once a sort of guide board past Prather's upper Island, rafts used to run quite near to it in order to go to the right of the Island, but both are now gone. The bar on which the Island stood is low and flat and of not much account in high water. It is situated a little above and extends down to the mouth of East Hickery Creek.

In rafting stages, Fishing bar is under water; in trying to run past it, as in former years, pilots have, some times, been deceived as to its precise location, and in some instances have run on to it or caught in the eddy water below the bar and swung.

Flat boats in very low water should keep near the ~~right~~ left shore when passing Green's landing and when down about the middle of the last Hemlock Islands turn short to the right. (See Chart.)

Rafts frequently go to the right of the Hemlock Islands but it is gennerly those that are made in Scott's Eddy on the right above the Island, the distance is greater besides the channel past the lowermost of the Islands being narrow and croocked.

Hemlock Eddy is on the left above the Islands. It is a very good eddy and sufficiently large to accomodate a number of fleets.

BEING in the immediate vicinity where the event transpired we will relate for the benefit of those who like to hear stories, a strange page in the history of an old Indian Chief of the Moncey tribe, by the name of Ross, and another Moncey by the name of Lock, who figured in this neighborhood as early as 1755 and probably earlier. The Monceys were a branch of the Delawares who had been crowded out from the Eastern waters by the encroachments of the whites, came to this region as early as 1724 which had been assigned them as a home by the Six Nations. But to return to the story :

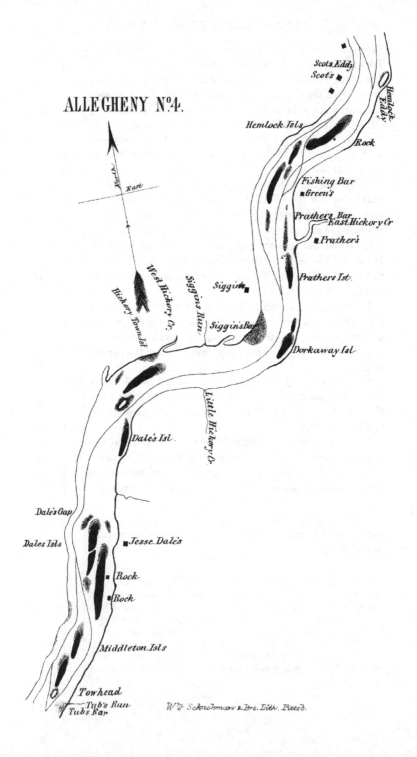

ALLEGHENY Nº 4.

North
East

Scots Eddy
Scot's
Hemlock Eddy
Hemlock Isls
Rock
Fishing Bar
Green's
Prathers Bar
East Hickory Cr
Prather's
West Hickory Cr.
Hickory Town Ist.
Siggin's Run
Siggins
Prathers Ist.
Siggin's Bar
Dorkaway Isl
Little Hickory Cr.
Dale's Isl.
Dale's Gap
Dale's Isls
Jesse Dale's
Rock
Rock
Middleton Isls
Towhead
Tub's Run
Tubs Bar

Wᵐ Schuchman & Bro. Lith. Pittsᵇ.

Ross and Lock, were in the employ of the British during the revolution-ary war. They together crossed the mountains on a trip for massacre and booty. Somewhere on the borders of Huntingdon, or Franklin Coun-ty they murdered in cold blood a Schoolmaster and twenty five or thirty children. Taking their scalps they proceded to Niagara, disposed of them and received the "bounty." Lock was somewhat of a bravado and on their return to Hickory Town represented himself as the principal hero of the scene. Ross was mortified and determined on revenge. In true Indian style he waited years for a uitable opportunity, and at last in a drunken war dance murdered Lock. This dance came off on the left side of the river out near the foot of the mountain not far from the mouth of East Hickory Creek. Lock it seems acted the part of singer, whiskey being in abundance, and Lock having twiged the bottle to the tune of a deep dram, became so stupefied that his music displeased Ross who commanded him several times to sing louder, but to no effect. Ross became enraged and seized a brand from the fire around which they were dancing and struck Lock on the head so hard that it put his music entirely out. Ross ap-peared before a council of the Senecas, and was condemned to support the widow of Lock for twenty years. At the expiration of that time he was to be slain by the nearest relative of Lock then living. This mild sen-tence was passed on account of his bravery. At the end of twenty years he surrendered himself up to the council of the tribe assembled near Buf-falo. In the mean time, the only son of Lock had married the daughter of Ross. His son-in-law was unwilling to slay him, for time had long since worn off the edge of his revenge, and so the sentence was never ex-ecuted. He lived to a great age and DIED on the banks of his native stream, the noble ALLEGHENY.

HICKORY TOWN ISLAND. - - - - - -   3¾   31½

Channel to the left; keep a little to the left of the middle til past the large tow-head at the foot of the Island, then make a long crossing to the right shore, to prepare for Dale's Gap. This will carry you clear of the bar at the head of Dale's up per Island, which lies close to the left shore.

The channel to the right of the Island is very shallow and frequently dry.

DALE'S ISLAND and GAP. * - ˏ - - - -   1¼   33¼

Channel to the right. Keep quite near the right shore around the right point while entering the Gap, and when past the large bar near the head of the Island, keep a little to the right of the middle till down to the foot, then turn rather short around the right shore point, to pass the head bar of Middle-ton's first Island, close by, and keep a little to the right of the middle till about half way down the second Island, which

* These directions extend below Hunter's Island, on to Map No. 5.

will carry you clear of its head bar, then turn out to the left so as to be close to the tow-head while passing it at the foot of the Island, and when past it, work over to the left, so as to pass about midway between Hunter's and May's Island. Turn a little to the left, while going down the riffle, to avoid the large bar on the right below the foot of Hunter's Island. When past the bars, cross over to the right shore to prepare for the Tionesta Islands.

At present, this track receives the most travel in all stages of water. But in low running it should not be done.

The channel to the left of the Middleton Islands is much deeper than to the right, and far better in low water. To run through this channel; while approaching the foot of Dale's Island, work to the left gradually, so as to be quite near the gravel bar at the foot. When past the bar, hold to the left, and pass about midway between the foot of Dale's long left hand Island and the head of Middleton's upper Island. And when down past the head of the second Middleton Island, incline to the right and run quite near the tow-head at the foot, to avoid Tubs' Bar, which makes out from the left at the mouth of Tubs' Run.

Flat boats in very low water should always take this channel.

The channel to the right of Hunter's Island has been for the last few years pretty generally deserted, and ought to have been many years ago.

It will be seen by the chart, that to the left of Dale's Islands would be like the Paddy's Jordan,—"a hard road to travel." It is very narrow, besides the two rocks being nearly one foot out of water in a rafting stage, to say nothing of the middle bar at the head of the Island.

DIRECTIONS FOR MAP NO. 5.

TIONESTA ISLANDS. - - - - - - - -	4¼	37½

Of these Islands there are thirteen in number, and extend down about two miles. Some of them are under a high state of cultivation and are owned by different Individuals.

ALLEGHENY N⁰ 5

Tionesta

Big Tionesta Cr.

Lit. Tionesta Cr.

Hunter's I.

Tionesta Isld.

Hendershun

Hunter's

Cushon Bars
Hollman's Eddy

Hunter's Run

North

East

Panther Run

Pierce's Run

Hollmans Isl.

Hollman's

Hollmans Bars

Hollman's Iowr'l

Maple Isls.

Wm. Schuchman & Bro. Lith. Pittsb.

Channel to the right. After passing the head of the second Island, keep near the middle till down about half way, past the main cluster, then work over gradually to the left and when past the head of the lower Island, hold to the left so as to run close to its foot, which will carry you clear of Cushon's bars on the right, which extend nearly to the foot of the Island; and from this point cross directly to the left shore; and while crossing, care should be taken not to be driven upon Cushon's Bars by the current that comes dowd the left of the Island. Flat boats and small pieces of lumber frequently go the left of these Island, but the channel is not wide enough for large rafts.

A short distance below the Islands, on the left, is Hollman's Eddy, a very good landing place for several fleets.

HOLLMAN'S ISLAND, - - - - - - - - -	$3\frac{1}{2}$	41

Channel to the left. About half way down the Island, is Hollman's Bars. In high running stages keep down close to the left shore, and to the left of the bars. But in very low water the best channel is to the right of the bars. When even with the head of the Island, keep out a little to the right of the middle, and when past the bars, turn back to the left a little above the head bar of Hollman's second Island. The water is not as deep by six inches to the left of Hollman's bars, as at Maple Island, although many think Maple Island to be the shallowest place on the river.

MAPLE ISLANDS. - - - - - - - - - -	1	42

Channel about mid way between the two that are on the right and the one close in to the left shore. While passing the lowermost Island on the right, keep about the middle, and also while approaching the bars in the bend below. The left of these is of no account in high water. When around the bend, cross to the right shore to prepare for Hemlock cr. Is.

DIRECTIONS FOR MAP NO. 6.

HEMLOCK CREEK ISLANDS. - - - - - -	$2\frac{1}{2}$	$44\frac{1}{2}$

The rafting channel is to the right. Keep down the right shore till bast all of the Islands, then cross to the left.

This channel is a little deeper than either of the others.

Flat boats, and the like, can go to the left of the first two Islands, and to the right of the two last. There is also a centre channel which is frequently navigated with boats. This is between the first two and to the right of the two last.

There are quite a number of metal boats loaded at this place during the year. These are generally loaded at Ralph Clapp's landing, and go down to the left of the first Islands.

Musk-Rat Eddy is a short distance below the foot of these Islands, on the left.

McCRAY'S ISLAND. - - - - - - - - - -	1¾	46¼

The main channel is to the left. From the foot of the Hemlock Creek Islands, keep near the left shore till past the towhead. There is also a channel between the Island and tow-head, but not generally used, except by those who want to land in the eddy below, on the right.

Henry's Bar is situated in the bend below, a little to the right of the middle, and opposite Henry's House. Channel to the left.

PITHOLE ISLAND and BARS. - - - - - -	2½	48¾

After passing Henry's Bar, cross to the right, and when going down Pithole riffle, keep quite near the right shore, to avoid a rough rocky bottom on the left, all along down the riffle. There is also a channel between the bars and Island, which is smoother but no deeper, and more difficult to navigate with large rafts.

WALNUT ISLANDS. - - - - - - - - - -	1½	50¼

The low water channel is to the right. But in fair running stages, the left is preferable. It is not as crooked, the distance also being less.

While approaching the Island on the left above, observe the strong current which makes to the right of the Island.

DOWNING'S BAR and HORSE CREEK EDDY.	2¾	53

This bar is so situated as to turn the main current of the river directly over to the left shore, and is therefore the prin-

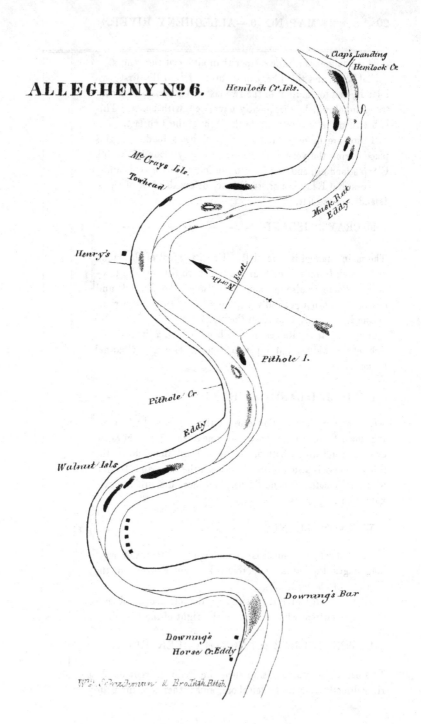

ALLEGHENY Nº 6.

cipal agent in forming Horse Creek Eddy, which lies immediately below the bar on the right, and is the usual landing place on the eve of the first day's run from Warren.

About sundown, rafts can be seen rounding into the eddy thick and three-fold. Both eddy and shore are literally alive with the Allegheny's "*Hardy Salts,* landing and securing their rafts for the night.

In order to pass to the left of the bar and land in the eddy, keep down about the middle of the river till past the head of the bar, then turn short to the right. This is the deepest, and safest channel, and is well calculated to extract the sweat from the boys. The Allegheny "Tars" are few and far between that are not willing to vouch for its diaphuretic qualities.

In very high water. rafts can go to the right of the bar, by keeping close to the right shore while running around the right point above, and land in the eddy with comparatively little labor. But this should never be attempted in anything like low running stages. Rafts sometimes land on the left, down about the Furnace.

DIRECTIONS FOR MAP NO. 7.

HORSE CREEK ISLAND. - - - - - - -   1¼   54¼

Channel to the right. After passing the foot of the Island keep nearest to the right shore till past Alcorn's Bars, which are a little to the left of the middle; the lowest of which is situated in the bend below.

OIL CREEK ISLAND, NO. I. - - - - ⟍ ⟍   3¼   57½

Channel to the right or left. In going to the right, after passing the head of the Island, run midling close to it to avoid the large bar on the right below the mouth of Oil Creek.

Oil Creek Eddy commences at the foot of the bar.

This is the place of embarkation for the Oil Creek lumber which is manufactured in great abundance for many miles up this stream.

OIL CREEK derives its name from a peculiar kind of inflamable oil known as the "Seneca Oil" which is found floating upon the surface of its waters in different places. This oil takes its name from the Seneca Indians. It was used by them as an unguent, and also in their religious worship. To the Indians it was almost as celebrated as the far famed

Neptha of the Caspian Sea. With it they mixed their war paint, which gave them a hideous glistening appearance and added great permanency to the paint, as it rendered it impervious to water. What a startling spectacle the oil anointed warrior of the Senecas must have been as he gave forth the fearful war-hoop or paddled his light canoe along the dark blue waters of the Allegheny. I will give a description of the use they made of this oil on one of their religious occasions in the language of the commandent of the Fort Duquesne in a letter to his Excellency Gen. Montcalm, the unfortunate hero of Quebec. This letter must have been written as early as 1753, in which the commandent says, "I would desire to assure your Excellency that this is a most delightful land. Some of the most astonishing natural wonders has been discovered by our people. While decending the Allegheny fifteen leagues below the mouth of the Conewango, and three above Fort Venango, we were invited by the Chief of the Senecas to attend a religous ceremony of his tribe. We landed and drew up our canoes on a point where a small stream entered the river.— The tribe appeared unusually solemn. We marched up the stream about a half league, where the company, a large band it appeared had arived some days before us. Gigantic hills begirt us on every side. The scene was really sublime. The great chief then recited the conquests and hero-ism of their ancestors. The surface of the stream was covered with a thick scum which bursts into a complete conflagration. The oil had been gathered and lighted by a torch. At the sight of the flames the Indians gave forth a triumphant shout, that made the hills and valleys reecho again! Here then is revived the ancient fire-workship of the East;— here then are the "Children of the Sun."

This oil has been discovered by the whites to possess several medicinal qualities, and is at present considered one of the valuables in Materia Medica.

The old Moncey chief 'Ross,' the hero of the Hickorytown dance confi-dently assured an aged citizen of Venango County that there were me-tals found and mines worked by the Senecas. And Black Snake a Seneca chief concurs in stating that there were three different mines between Franklin and Conewango, one of which is situated not far from the mouth of the creek. Any person who has traveled over the road between Franklin and Oil Creek will remember a deep dark ravine overhung with rocks, hemlock and pine, about a quarter of a mile below Hollidays.— Ross led the white man up the ravine about a hundred and twenty rods : there another gulf comes down from the right, up which they passed some fifty rods further. The gap here assumes a fearfully dark' and forbiding appearance. Vast rocks are thrown and piled one upon another, and the hill has the appearance of having been rent by an earthquake. The chief here bid the white man stop, and mentioning the awful death inflicted on one who disclosed the mines to strangers, said, "I can go no farther. This mine is within five rods of here—find it for your self." At the same time he showed several specimens of metal procured there. It was of an excelent quality though poorly refined. The mineral was found as in South America, in sand-stone rock. This spot has been a familiar one to Cornplanter. Some time about 1792, the Commonwealth of Pennsylvania granted him a tract of about 500 acres of land here, including the oil springs; which he sold many years ago. A fuller and more concise histo-ry of this distinguished individual will be found in the history of Franklin.

OIL CREEK ISLAND NO. 2. - - - - - -	1	58½

Channel to the right. From the foot of the Island, keep about three-fourths of the river to the left, till nearly around the bend below, which is about one mile, then incline over to the left shore. This will carry you clear of Holliday's Bars at the head of the bend on the left.

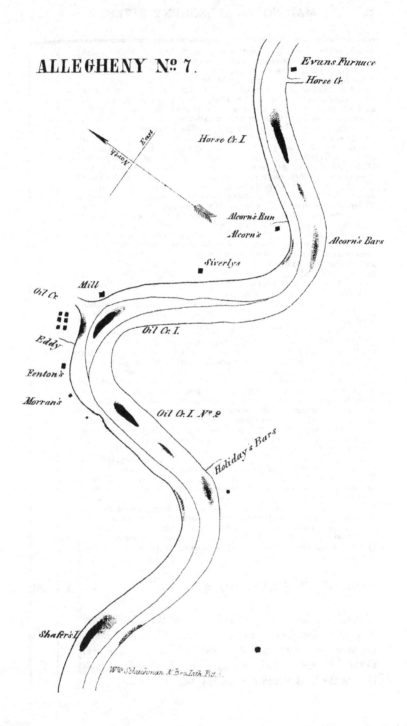

ALLEGHENY № 7.

Evans Furnace
Horse Cr.

Horse Cr. I.

North East

Alcorn's Run
Alcorn's

Alcorn's Bars

Siverlys

Oil Cr. Mill

Oil Cr. I.

Eddy

Fenton's

Morran's

Oil Cr. I. № 2

Holiday's Bars

Shafers I.

Wm Schuchman & Bro. Lith. Pitt.

ALLEGHENY № 8.

2 Mile Run
2 Mile R. I.

French Cr.

Dam

Lock

McDowell's I.

Old Garrison Bar
T. Ridgways

Bridge

Blue Rocks Bar

2 Mile Run

Blue Rock

3 Mile I.

Beck's Riffle

North   East

4 Mile I.

Smith's Bar

Big Sandy Cr.

Foster's I.
Smiths

Big Sandy Eddy

East Sandy Cr.

Hanging Rock Bar
& Riffle

Indian God
Bar made by Ice in 1855

Manson's Bar's

Applegate's Riffle

Witherup's Bar

Witherup's

Steen's I.
Charly's Riffle
& Bars.

Wm Schuchman & Bro. Lith. Pittsb.

SHAFER'S ISLAAND. - - - - - - - - -	3	61½

Channel to the left. Keep a little to the left of the middle of the chute while passing the head bar of the Island.

DIRECTIONS FOR MAP NO. 8.

TWO MILE RUN ISLAND. - - - - - - -	1	62½

Channel to the left, a little to the left of the middle of the chute.

McDOWELL'S ISLAND. - - - - - - - - -	1¼	63¾

Channel to the left. Keep about the middle till down to the foot, which will place you in about the right distance from the left shore, to run around the bend and pass through the third space from the right shore to Franklin Bridge.

Small rafts and flat boats can go down to the right, by keeping near the right shore after passing the two mile run Island. In order to land in Franklin for the purpose of doing business any where near the business part of the town, it will be necessary to take this channel and cross the mouth of French Creek.

In high water, boats can be landed any where between the bridge and lock, there being plenty of water on Old Garrison Bar, but in low water it will be necessary to land either below the bar, and a little above the Bridge, or at the upper Steam Boat landing. a few rods below the lock. The upper landing is performed by towing up, either before or after crossing the mouth of French Creek.

A few years ago Old Garrison Bar was covered with soil and was the main shore. The Old Garrison spoken of in the history of Foanklin, stood directly upon it.

FRANKLIN, the seat of justice for Venango County, is situated on a broad plain a little above the mouth of French Creek, and is surrounded with scenery highly picturesque. The distance from Pittsburgh by water is 139 miles, by land being only 68 miles. It contains the usual county buildings and Presbyterian, Methodist and Cumberland Presbyterian Churches. Franklin is evidently built rong end to, which can be accounted for in the following manner: In the spring of 1787 a company of U.

S. troops under the command of Capt. Hart arrived at this place from Fort Pitt, now Pittsburgh. They amounted to 87 in number, including officers. There were perhaps a dozen other persons not immediately connected with the corps, and this constituted the whole board at that time. Immediately on their arrivle they commenced erecting what they called Fort Franklin, and from which the name of the Town is derived. In place of locating it at the mouth of French creek so as to command that stream as well as the Allegheny river, they made their location about 180 rods above the mouth of the former, and at a point that would not at all command the latter. The road from Fort Pitt to Le Bœuf, now Waterford, crossed the creek within a few rods of the fort, and had as the reason may appear, it was perhaps the only one that induced the selection. It was a mere Indian path then, but the fording was good, and the assent of the oposite hill was the most practicable from it. Indeed the existance of this path, and the erection of the fort near it, induced those who settled here at an early period to make their location near to both these supposed advantages. The road, or path, was the only inland thoroughfare to the place, and on it, in the town, was established the hotel and near this the merchant erected his stall, and the mechanic his shop.— Thus was the town at that time built upon its present site, far from where strangers think it ought to have been located.

Fort Franklin was located immediately above, and west of the south end, of the French creek bridge, and consequently on the south bank of French Creek. It was a parallelogram, the out works including about 100 feet square. These works consisted of high embankments, outside of which arose tall pine pickets 16 feet high. There were four bastions surmounted by small cannon. Within the area formed by the ditches, was the block house with a huge stack of chimneys in the center. In this building were the magazine and munitions. The huts of the soldiers were in the ditch around the block house and within the pickets. This fort was situated on a bluff bank of the creek 25 or 30 feet high and nearly perpendicular. To this day is to be seen a deep ditch running along the top and near the edge of this bank some 120 feet in length up the creek. This was intended for a covered way leading from the fort to a small redoubt ot the very margin of the creek, which was mounted by two guns. The garrison had what they called a green house, or cave, in which they kept vegetables and meat. This was within a few feet of the excavation made at the end of the bridge for a toll house. A garrison of nearly 100 men, including officers, was kept at Fort Franklin until 1796 when, what is familiarly known as the 'Old Garrison,' at the mouth of the creek, was erected by the troops at the Fort, at a point more convenient for receiving provisions and munitions brought up by boats and canoes from Pittsburgh. It was a strong wooden building, a story and a half high and, perhaps 30, by 34 feet in length. It was picketed in, but not calculated to be mounted with cannon. Indeed the necessity for this had ceased as as the treaty of Gen. Wayne with the Indians at Fort Greenville had been made in 1795 and was then believed, as it turned out to be, a lasting peace. From the time the troops occupied che garrison, the Fort was suffered to dilapidate, and went entirely to ruins. The stone in the chimneys was hauled away by the estizens of the place, and used in building foundations and chimneys for private dwellings. The Troops continued to occuy the garrison untill 1803 when they were withdrawn from Frank-

lin altogether. The "Old Garrison" was occupied from the organization
of the county in 1805 as a common jail, when the new county jail was
completed. It remained standing, though in ruins, until 1824, when the
last vestage disappeared, and the very foundation on which it stood was
washed away and is now a part of the bed of French Creek.

There are also the remains of two other forts here of a more ancient
date, and erected at different periods. These were located just below the
junction of French Creek, so as to command the Allegheny. The most
ancient of the two, the people of the villiage call the Old French Fort.—
Its ruins plainly indicate its destruction by fire. Burnt stone, melted
glass and iron, leave no doubt of this. All through the groundworks are
to be found mouldering bones, knives, gun-barrels, locks, musket-balls,
&c. M. De Lignery, the French commander, no doubt burned the works
here as he had done those at Fort Duquesne in 1759 when they withdrew
their forces at this place, Le Bœuf and Presqu'isle, to strengthen Fort
Niagara. This fort was situated a short distance below the Franklin
bridge. The other, *Fort Venango* or the *Old English Fort*, so called, is
situated about oposite and a short distance from the right end of the
bridge. It was the prevailing opinion that this fort was built by the
English, after the close of the French and Indian war. But there are no
records of this post being garrisoned by the British at all. At the time of
the famous war of Pontiac in 1763 no mention is made of any garrison at
Venango by the early writers in their catalogue of places invested by the
Indian forces. It is highly probable that this ancient piece of work was
built by the French after the destruction of the first one, for neither history nor tradition furnishes us with any name or number of Englishmen
ever being here. The remains of this work are still very distinct. From
the top of the embankment to the bottom of the ditch is yet about eight
feet in depth. There were four bastions that commanded all the angles
of the fort. The fortification was square each side being about 100
feet. Inside of the embankment was a deep ditch, and within the area
formed by the ditch, was situated the block house and magazine. From
the south east corner of the fort was a subterranean passage to a little
stream that passes within 150 feet of it. Here a dam had been erected,
the foundation timbers still exists. This subterranean passage, was undoubtedly made for a cover, by which means water could be procured with
safety, and also for the purpose of filling the ditches around the block
house, surrounding it with a formidable barrier of water 6 or 7 feet deep
and twice that wide. The northern angle of the breast-works has been
almost entirely removed to construct the embankment at the west end of
the bridge.

"That these works had cannon on them, cannot be doubted, as a small
one, perhaps a four-pounder, was found in the bank of the river some four
or five years ago. The old gun, which doubtless had withstood the shock
of contending foes—had survived the discomfort of *savage* association, and
while a century of storm, of sunshine, of flood a..d tide, had rolled away,
had lain snug, hale, and hearty, in its place of security—was at last discovered by some people, who dragged it from its resting-place, and *with
their advantage in science* over its old masters, loaded it to the muzzle
with *powder and sand*, and—*blew it to pieces!* It is a wonder that its
last loud and *parting* peal did not awaken from his deep slumber some
old friend to avenge the indignity !"

"A few rods northeast of the fort, near Franklin, are a great number of graves. These are the long-homes of the soldier and the savage. They are not the graves of whitemen alone, for some of the citizens a few years since opened several of them, and found Indian remains and arms. This custom of burying arms, clothing, or culinary vessels, with the deceased, prevailed not among the French or English, but among the Indians alone. It was a pleasant and enchanting spot to lie down in that "sleep that knows no waking." There come the Allegheny and French Creek, and mingle their waters, like streams of life flowing on to the gulf of eternity. Who shall tell the story of the sleepers in these narrow habitations? None! No column, no stone, however lowly, tells a letter of their history. Yet there sleep men who once engaged in the bloody struggle for universal empire, in the eighteenth century, between the Bourbon and the Britain. There are many graves scattered throughout the county. On the summit of the hill above the dam, there is the grave undoubtedly of some great chief. The excavation is unusually deep, and great care and labor have been expended in its construction. It occupies a commanding position. The town, stream, and landscape around are seen to great advantage from this point. With anxious eye the aged chief has cast a dying glance on the home of his childhood and age, and the wigwams of his people below, and then composed himself in death on the summit of this hill. His grave is like the grave of the great chieftain of Israel, made amidst the rocks and solitude of the mountain. In the wild and poetic religion of the Indian, the spirit of the warrior was often seen upon that lonely hill, like some sleepless sentinel pointing out to his tribe the path of safty and glory.

FEW names are more distinguished in the frontier history of Pennsylvania, than that of CORNPLANTER. People who have traveled up and down the Allegheny river, will recollect of having seen Cornplanter Stables, Hotels, Steamboats, etc., in short, a great many Cornplanter things. In order to inform the reader of the origin and source of all of this apelation timber, we will give a short account of his birth, parentage, and a portion of his general life. He was born in Conewagus, on the Genessee river. His Indian name was *Ga-nio-di-euh* or *Handsome Lake*. He was only a half breed, the son of a white man named John O'Bail, a trader from the Mohawk Valley. In a letter written in latter years to the Governor of Pennsylvania, he thus speaks of his early youth.

"When I was a child, I played with the butterfly, the grasshopper, and the frogs; and as I grew up, I began to pay some attention and play with the Indian boys in the neighborhood; and they took notice of my skin being of a different color from theirs, and spoke about it. I inquired of my mother the cause, and she told me that my father was a resident in Albany. I still ate my victuals out of a bark dish. I grew up to be a young man, and married me a wife, and I had no kettle or gun. I then knew where my father lived, and went to see him, and found he was a white man and spoke the English language. He gave me victuals while I was at his house, but when I started to return, he gave me no provisions to eat by the way. He gave me neither kettle nor gun."   *   *   *

Little further is known of his early life, beyond the fact that he was al lied with the French in the engagement against Gen. Braddock in 1755. He was probably at that time, at least twenty years old. During the revolution he was a war chief, of high rank, in the full vigor of manhood, active, sagacious, eloquent, and brave ; and he most probably participated in the principal Indian engagements against the United States during the war. He is supposed to have been present at the cruelties of Wyoming and Cherry Valley, in which the Senecas took a prominent part. He was on the war path with Brant during Gen. Sullivan's campaign, in 1779; and in the following year, under Brant and Sir John Johnson, he led the Senecas in sweeping through the Schoharie Kill and the Mohawk. On this occasion he took his father a prisoner, but with such caution as to avoid an immediate recognition. After marching the old man some ten or twelve miles, he stepped before him, faced about, and addressed him in the following terms:

"My name is John O'Bail, commonly called Cornplanter. I am your son! You are my father ! You are my prisoner, and subject to the customs of Indian warfare. But you shall not be harmed. You need not fear. I am a warior ! Many are the scalps which I have taken ! many have I tortured to death ! I am your son. I was anxious to see you, and greet you in friendship. I went to your cabin, and took you by force; but your life shall be spared. Indians love their friends and their kindred, and treat them with kindness. If you choose to follow the fortunes of your yellow son, and to live with our people, I will cherish your old age with plenty of venison, and you shall live easy. But if it is your choice to return to your fields and live with your white children, I will send a party of my trusty young men to conduct you back in safty. I respect you, my father. You have been friendly to Indians, and they are your friends." The elder O'Bail preferred his white children and green fields to his yellow offspring and the wild woods, and chose to return.

Notwithstanding his bitter hostility while the war continued, he became a fast friend of the United States when once the hatchet was buried. His sagacious intellect comprehended at a glance the growing power of the United States, and the abandonment with which Great Britain had requited the fidelity of the Senecas. He therefore threw all his influence, at the treaties of Fort Stanwix and Fort Harmar, in favor of peace ; and, notwithstanding the vast concessions which he saw his people were necessitated to make, still, by his energy and prudence in the negotiation, he retained for them an ample and beautiful reservation. For the course which he took on those occasions the State of Pennsylvania granted him the fine reservation upon which he resided, on the Allegheny. The Senecas, however, were never well satisfied with his course in relation to these treaties; and Red Jacket, more artful and eloquent than his elder rival, but less frank and honest, seized upon this circumstance to promote his own popularity at the expense of Cornplanter.

Having buried the hatchet, Cornplanter sought to make his talents useful to his people by conciliating the good will of the whites, and securing from further encroachment the little remnant of his national domain. On more than one occasion, when some reckless and bloodthirsty whites on the frontier had massacred unoffending Indians in cold blood, did Cornplanter interfere to restrain the vengeance of his people. During all the Indian wars from 1791 to 1794, which terminated with Wayne's treaty, Cornplanter pledged himself that the Senecas should remain friendly to the United States. He often gave notice to the garrison at Fort Franklin of intended attacks from hostile parties, and even hazarded his life on a mediatorial mission to the Western tribes. He ever entertained a high respect and personal frienpship for Gen. Washington, "the great councillor of the Thirteen Fires," and often visited him during his presidency, on the business of his tribe. His speeches on these occasions exhibit both his talent in composition and his adroitness in diplomacy. Washington fully reciprocated his respect and friendship. They had fought against each other on the disasterous day of Braddock's field. Both were then young men. More than forty years afterwards, when Washington was about retiring from the presidency, Cornplanter made a special visit to Philadelphia to take an affectionate leave of the great benefactor of the white man and the red.

After peace was permanently established between the Indians and the United States, Cornplanter retired from public life, and devoted his labors to his own people. He deplored the evils of intemperance, and exerted himself to suppress it. The benevolent efforts of missionaries among his tribe always received his encouragement, and at one time his own heart seemed to be softened by the words of truth ; yet he preserved, in his latter years, many of the peculiar notions of the Indian faith.

In 1821-2 the commissioners of Warren county assumed the right to tax the private property of Cornplanter, and proceeded to enforce its collection. The old chief resisted it, conceiving it not only unlawful, but a personal indignity. The sheriff again appeared with a small posse of armed men. Cornplanter took the deputation to a room around which were ranged about a hundred rifles, and, with the sententious brevity of an Indian, intimated that for each rifle a warrior would appear at his call. The sheriff and his men speedily withdrew, determined, however, to call out the militia. Several prudent citizens, fearing a sanguinary collision, sent for the old chief in a friendly way to come to Warren and compromise the matter. He came, and after some persuasion, gave his note for the tax, amounting to $43,79. He addressed, however, a remonstrance to the Gov. of Pennsylvania, soliciting a return of his money, and an exemption from such demands against land which the state itself had presented to him.— The legislature annulled the tax, and sent two commissioners to explain the affair to him. He met them at Warren, on which occasion he delivered the following speech, eminently characteristic of himself and his race :

"Brothers : Yesterday was appointed for us all to meet here. The talk which the governor sent us pleased us very much. I think the Great Spirit is very much pleased that the white people have been induced so to assist the Indians as they have done, that he is pleased also to see the great men of this state and of the United States so friendly to us. We are much pleased with what has been done.

"The Great Spirit first made the World, and next the flying animals, and found all things good and prosperous. He is immortal and everlasting. After finishing the flying animals, he came down on earth and there stood. Then he made different kinds of trees, and weeds of all sorts, and people of every kind. He made the spring and other seasons, and the weather suitable for planting. These he did make. But stills to make whiskey to be given to Indians he did not make. The Great Spirit bids me tell the white people not to give Indians this kind of liquor. When the Great Spirit had made the earth and its animals, he went into the great lakes, where he breathed as easy as anywhere else, and then made all the different kinds of fish. The Great Spirit looked back on all that he

had made. The different kinds he made to be separate, and not mix with
and disturb each other. But the white people have broken his command
by mixing their color with the Indians. The Indians have done better by
not doing so. The Great Spirit wishes that all wars and fightings should
cease.

"He next told us that there were three things for our people to attend
to. First, we ought to take care of our wives and children. Secondly,
the white people ought to attend to their farms and cattle. Thirdly, the
Great Spirit has given the bears and deers to the Indians. He is the cause
of all things that exist, and it is very wicked to go against his will. The
Great Spirit wishes me to inform the people that they should quit drinking intoxicating drink, as being the cause of disease and death. He told
us not to sell any more of our lands, for he never sold lands to any one.
Some of us now keep the seventh day; but I wish to quit it, for the Great
Spirit made it for others, but not for Indians, who ought every day to attend to their business. He has ordered me to quit drinking any intoxicating drink, and not to lust after any woman but my own, and informs me
that by doing so I should live the longer. He made known to me that it
is very wicked to tell lies. Let no one suppose this I have said is not true.

"I have now to thank the governor for what he has done. I have informed him what the Great Spirit has ordered me to cease from, and I
wish the governor to inform others of what I have communicated. This
is all I have at present to say."

The old chief appears after this again to have fallen into entire seclusion,
taking no part even in the politics of his people. He died at his residence
on the 7th March, 1836, at the age of 100 years and upwards. Whether
at the time of his death he expected to go to the fair hunting grounds of
his own people, or to the heaven of the Christian, is unknown.

Notwithstanding his profession of Christianity, Cornplanter was very
superstitious. "Not long since," says Mr. Foote, of Chautauque co., "he
said the Good Spirit had told him not to have anything to do with the
white people, or even to preserve any mementoes or relics that had been
given to him, from time to time, by the pale-faces,—whereupon, among
other things, he burnt up his belt, and broke his elegant sword."

In refference to the personal appearance of Cornplanter at the close of
his life, a writer in the Democratic Arch, (Venango co.,) says:—

"I once saw the aged and venerable chief, and had an interesting in-
terview with him about a year and a half before his death. I thought of
many things when seated near him, beneath the wide spreading shade of
an old Sycamore, on the banks of the Allegheny—many things to ask
him—the scenes of the revolution, the generals that fought its battles and
conquered the Indians, his tribe, the Six Nations and himself. He was
constitutionally sedate,—was never observed to smile, much less to indulgd
in the 'luxury of a laugh.' When I saw him, he estimated his age to be
over 100 years. I think 103 was about his reckoning of it. This would
make him near 105 years old at the time of his decease. His person was
much stooped, and his stature was far short of what it once had been—not
being over 5 feet 6 inches at the time I speak of. Mr. John Struthers, of
Ohio, told me, some years since, that he had seen him near 50 years ago,
and at that period he was about his height—viz: 6 feet 1 inch. Time and
hardship had made dreadful impressions upon that ancient form. The
chest was sunken, and his shoulders were drawn forward, making the up-

per part of his body resemble a trough. His limbs had lost their size and become crooked. His feet, too, (for he had taken off his moccasins,) were deformed and haggard by injury. I would say that most of the fingers on one hand were useless : the sinews had been severed by a blow of the toma-hawk or scalping knife. How I longed to ask him what scene of blood and strife had thus stamped the enduring evidence of its existence upon his person ! But to have done so would, in all probability, have put an end to all further conversation on any subject,—the information desired would certainly not have been received, and I had to forego my curiosity. He had but one eye, and even the socket of the lost organ was hid by the overhanging brow resting upon the high cheek-bone. His remaining eye was of the brightest and blackest hue. Never have I seen one in young or old, that equalled its brilliancy. Perhaps it had borrowed lustre from the eternal darkness that rested on its neighboring orb. His ears had been dressed in the Indian mode : all but the outside ring had been cut away. On one ear this ring had been tore asunder near the top, and hung down his neck like a useless rag. He had a full head of hair, white as the 'driven snow,' which covered a head of ample dimensions and admirable shape. His face was not swarthy ; but this may be accounted for from the fact, also, that he was but half Indian. He told me that he had been at Frank-lin more than 80 years before the period of our conversation, on his pas-sage down the Ohio and Mississippi with the warriors of his tribe, on some expedition against the Creeks and Osages. He had long been a man of peace, and I believe his great characteristics were humanity and truth. It is said that Brant and Cornplanter were never friends after the massa-cre of Cherry Valley. Some have alleged; because the Wyoming massacre was perpetrated by the Senecas, that Cornplanter was there. Of the jus-tice of this suspicion there are many reasons for doubt It is certain that he was not the chief of the Senecas at that time : the name of the chief in that expedition was Ge-en-quah-toh, or He-goes-in-the-smoke. As he stood before me, the ancient chief in ruins, how forcibly was I struck with the truth of the beautiful figure of the old aboriginal chieftain, who, in de-scribing himself, said he was 'like an aged hemlock dead at the top, and whose branches alone were green.' After more than one hundred years of most varied life—of strife, of danger, and of peace—h? at last slumbers in deep repose, on the banks of his own beloved Allegheny."

FRANKLIN BRIDGE. - - - - - - - - -	1¼	65

There are three piers to the bridge and rafts that go down to the left of McDowell's Island should always take the third space from the right shore. After passing the bridge keep near the middle down to Blue Rock Bars.

BLUE ROCK BARS. - - - - - - - - -	1	66

These bars are situated in the bend below, one on the right, and one on the left. Channel between, and a little to the left of the middle of the river. When past these bars, keep near the middle, and when going down Becks Riffle, incline to the right to prepair for the

THREE MILE ISLAND. - - - - - - - - -	1½	67½

Channel to the right. Keep quite near the right shore while passing the large gravel bar that lays along side of the Island; when past the foot, cross to the left to prepare for the

FOUR MILE ISLAND. - - - - - - - - -	1½	69

Channel to the left. When down to the foot of this Island incline over to the right shore to go to the right of Smith's Bar about three-fourths of a mile below and while passing from the foot of this bar, keep three-fourths of the river to the left till below the mouth of East Sandy Creek, then make a long crossing to the left shore. This will carry you clear of the bar below the mouth of East Sandy Creek on the left.

FOSTER'S ISLAND. - - - - - - - - - -	3¼	72½

Channel to the left. At the foot of the Island commences the Manson's Bars, which extend down to the Indian God rock. Keep about midway between the bars and the left shore, and when past the head of the lowermost bar, in low water, incline to the right, and keep close to it, till down to the foot, which is about even with the Indian God rock.—Then cross directly over to the right shore to pass around the bar made by ice in 1854. This bar makes out from the left shore a little below the Indian God. It is of no account in high water, rafts run directly over it.

This remarkable rock, known as the *Indian God*, stands on the left margin of the river near to the waters edge. It undoubtedly records the history, exploits and illusstrious actions of departed and forgotten nations and their battles for the space of many hundred years. Among the figures carved upon it can be distinguishesd a snake, an eye, a turtle, an arrow and a sun. Among the more prominent there are some, which bear a slight resemblance to the human species, and different parts of the human frame. These are symbols or hieroglyphics. They appear to have been indented into the surface of the rock with some rude pointed instrument.—Who shall decipher and translate these wonderous characters

HANGING ROCK BAR and RIFFLE. - - - -	4	76½

Channel to the right or left. The easiest and best channel is to the left, when nearly down to the mouth of Big Sandy Creek which comes in on the right above, incline over to the left shore, and when past the bar cross to the right. This channel should always be run except when leaving Big Sandy Eddy, in which case it should not be attempted with a large raft. Flat boats can cross from the eddy to the left of the bar very easily. After passing the bar keep near the right shore down to

APPLEGATE'S RIFFLE and WITHERUP S BARS.	¾	77¼

Channel to the right. Keep near the right shore while go ing down the riffle, and when down to the foot of the bars prepare to go either to the right or left of Steen's Island.

STEEN'S ISLAND. - - - - - - - - - -	1½	78¾

Channel to the right or left. The deepest water is to the right but the main rafting track is to the left in almost every stage of water, it being about as deep to the left as it is on Applegate's or Charley's riffles, after passing the Island keep near the right shore to prepare for

CHARLEY'S RIFFLE and BARS. - - - - -	1¼	80

Channel to the right. Keep near the right shore while going down the riffle and when around the bend incline over to the left to prepare for Williams' Bars.

- - - - - -

DIRECTIONS FOR MAP NO. 9.

WILLIAMS' BARS. - - - - - - - - -	1¾	81¾

Channel to the left. These bars are situated about three-fourths of a mile above the mouth of Denison's run which comes in on the right, in passing them keep about three-fourths of the river to the right and when past them incline over to the right to prepare for

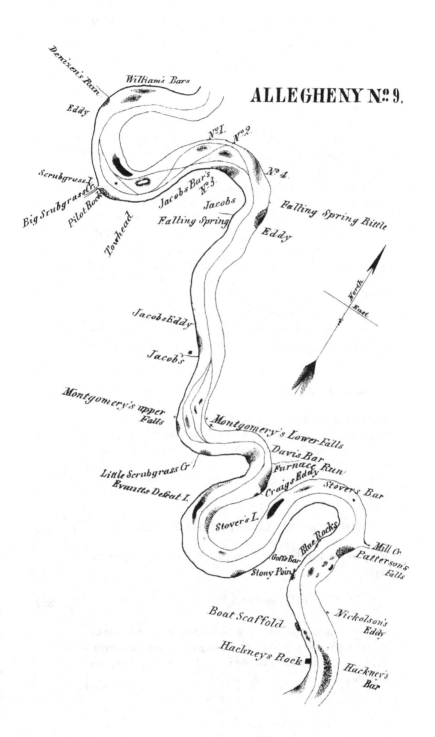

ALLEGHENY Nº 9.

BIG SCRUBGRASS ISLAND and BARS. - - -	1¾	83¼

There are three channels here all of which are to the right of the Island. The one generally used and probably under all circumstances the safest, is the right shore channel and to the right of Pilot rock. This channel is rather hard to run in consequence of there being a heavy press of water to the right shore below Pilot rock.

The second, or middle channel, is between the Pilot rock and the tow-head. This channel is the deepest, and requires less work but more skill to navigate it. To go through it with a large raft, be a little to the right of the middle of the river while going down the reach above, and then as the saying is "keep your eye well skined" on the draft of water and not run upon the Pilot rock, nor the tow-head on the left and a little below.

The third, or channel between the tow-head and foot of the Island, is not safe for large rafts but is very good for flat boats. After passing these bars keep near the right shore to prepare for

JACOB'S BARS. - - - - - - - - - -	2	85½

The deepest and best channel is to the right of bar No. 1 and No. 2, then cross to the left to avoid bar No. 3, which makes out from the right shore part way around the bend, then cross back to the right to avoid bar No. 4.

The extreme left channel is a narrow one dug by the keel boatmen.

JACOB'S, or FALLING SPRING RIFFLE. - -	1	86½

Eddy on the left below the riffle. Falling Spring on the right.

JACOB'S EDDY, on the right. - - - - - - -	2¼	88¾

Large bar in the eddy, rafts in high water frequently tie up for the night directly over it, although not very safe, especially when the water is falling fast. After leaving this place prepare for

MONTGOMERY'S FALLS and ELEPHANT BARS	1½	90¼

There are three channels here. In low water, while passing
the Elephant bars, at the upper falls, keep the right shore
channel, when down to the foot of the riffle, incline to the left
and run down about the middle of the lower falls

In high water keep close to the left shore while passing
the bars, then incline to the middle.

The center channel is wider, and a little deeper than the
left channel.

DAVIS' BAR. - - - - - - - - - - - -	1½	91¾

This bar makes out from the right shore point, in the bend,
and reaches over half way across the river. In good running
stages, it is of not much account. Keep a little to the left
of the middle while passing it. But in low water run around
quite near the left shore.

Craig's Eddy is just below on the left.

EVAULT'S DEFEAT ISLAND. - - - - - -	1½	93¼

Channel to the left. In low water, keep near the head of the
Island when passing it, to avoid a rough, rocky bottom along
the left of the riffle, and when about two-thirds down the riffle,
graduly incline to the left.

In a good running stage, go down about the middle.

To the right of the Island it is frequently dry.

STOVER'S ISLAND. - - - - - - - - - -	2½	95¾

Channel to the right. This island lays quite near the left
shore. When down to the foot, keep about two thirds of the
river to the left, till past Stover's bar, immediately below the
Island.

PATTERSON'S FALLS. - - - - - - - - -	2	97¾

Keep down about the middle, and when down to the foot,
keep near the right shore to pass to the right of Goff's Bar a
short distance below.

This bar is situated in the middle of the river, and a little above a small stony point on the right shore. In low running stages, it is a little under water, and well calculated to deceive. Look out for it.

When going around the bend below, incline to the right shore to prepare for

NICHOLSON'S EDDY and HACKNEY'S BAR.	2	99¾

Channel to the right. When down even with the little right shore bar, a few rods below the boat scaffold, turn in a little more to the right, to pass the head of Hackney's bar, and then incline more to the left. The head of the bar extends up so near the little one on the right, below the boat scaffold, as only to leave a narrow pass sufficient to slip through, which must be done in season, for the main current of the river at this point crosses directly to the left of the bar, and then spreads over the bar for the space of over half of a mile back into the right channel again. The bar is about a mile long. When down near the foot, cross directly to the left shore to avoid a rocky bar on the right point.

Tradition says, Nicholsons Eddy derived its name from a mistake made by the pilot of a keel boat, in an early period of keel boating on the Allegheny river.

The Pilot, whose name was Nicholson, on arriving within sight of the bend below the riffle, told his men who had been labouring hard all day, they would have easy times, when they got up to that bend, for it was still water for several miles but what was there supprise on reaching the bend, to find *swift water* for nearly two miles. They however got up a hearty laugh at the pilots expence and called it Nicholsons Eddy, a name which it is known by to this day.

DIRECTIONS FOR MAP NO. 10.

EMLENTON and BRIDGE. - - - - - - -	3	102¾

The bridge has but one pier, and that stands in the middle of the river. Channel to the right.

In going past Emlenton it will require more or less care
to keep from rubing the rocks along the right shore, till down
to the rocky point, below the town at the head of Ritchies
Riffle.

EMLENTON, situated on the left, has arrived to the digni-
ty of quite a commercial place. It contains the usual supply of mechanics shops, and stores. Messrs. Brown, Floyd
&. Co, of Pittsburgh have an extensive iron store here, besides there are several other mercantile establishments.—
Large quantities of grain are annually shipped from this to
foreign ports.

On the right, and about one-fourth of a mile above the bridge,
Dr. Bishop is doing an extensive mercantile business, and
also in furnishing the Pittsburgh glass manufactories with
sand-stone. On the whole, this is quite a point for trade.

CUMMINGS' TRUNK RIFFLE and CRAWFORD'S BAR. ⟍ - - ⟍ - - - ⟍ - - - - - - - -	2	104¼

Channel to the right. Keep a little to the right of the middle while passing the bar which lays quite near the left shore.

STUMP CREEK EDDY, on the left. - ⟍ - ⟍ -	2	106¾

This or Miller's Eddy is the usual place of landing, on the
second night after leaving Warren.

STUMP CREEK ISLANDS. - - - - ⟍ - - ⸱⸱	1½	108¾

Rafting channel to the left In very low water, when past
the head of the bar to the Second Islands, keep a little out from
the left shore, to avoid the rocky bottom, on the left, above
the mouth of the Clarion; then turn rather short in to the
mouth of the Creek, and then out again, then keep near the
left shore till past the middle of the third Island, a bar from
which makes out over half way to the left shore.

The low water boat channel is to the right of the two first
Islands. Cross back into the left channel again, close to the
foot of the second Island. This channel is not safe for rafts.

In high water Flat boats can go to the right of the third
Island.

Parker's landing is on the right, Graham's on the left, just
below this Island.

ALLEGHENY N.º 10.

Emlinton

Ritchie's Run

Ritchie's Riffle

Doctor Bishops Store

Bridge

Rocky Point

Lowrie's Run

Cumming's Trunk Riffle

Crawfords Bar

Stamp Cr. Eddy

Colgins

Reddick's Run

North

East

Stamp Cr. Isls.

Clairon River

Graham's Landing

Parkers Landing

Parker's Bars

Parkers Run

Parker's Falls

Bear Cr.

Rattelsnake Falls

Soap Run

Wm Schuchman & Bro. Lith. Pittsb.

PARKER'S BARS.	2¼	110½

The main rafting track in good running stages, is down the left, and about midway between the bar and left shore. The center channel is the deepest and best in low water. Flat boats can go to the right of the little bar opposite the mouth of Parker's run, and a little below Parker's landing.

PARKER'S FALLS.	¾	111¼

Channel about the middle.

RATTLE SNAKE FALLS.	1¼	112½

Bar on the right, and left. Channel about the middle.

DIRECTIONS FOR MAP NO. 11.

MILLER'S EDDY, on the right.	2¾	115¼

This excellent Eddy is formed by a large bar that makes out from the right shore, and turns the current out towards the middle of the river. In high water it is two days run from Warren. This is also a considerable of a place of business.— Manufactoring of fire brick is extensively carried on here.

BLACK FOX ISLAND.	¾	116

Channel to the right. In low water keep out towards the Island, till past the bar on the right, below the saw mill — Then turn to the right to avoid the large bar that makes out from the head of the Island.

BALD EAGLE ISLAND.	1¼	117¼

Channel to the right,

ARMSTRONG'S RAPIDS, or TRUBY'S RIFFLE and **TRUBY'S BARS.**	2¾	120

In good running stages, when around Cinder Bank Bend, keep down the left shore. Some rocks in the water about three rods from the left shore, at the head of the riffle.

In very low water, keep down about the middle of the river
and pass between the middle bar, and the long flat shore bar on
the right. Turn a little to the right while going down between the bars.

Good Eddy in the bend below, on the right.

CATFISH FALLS. - - - - - - - - - -   2¼   122¼

Keep about two thirds of the river to the left, at the commencement of the riffle, to pass between the middle bar, and
the mill-dam, on the right.

The low water boat channel, is down the left shore, and to
the left of the middle bar, and quite near the mouth of Catfish run.

Catfish Eddy on the left, below the large shore bar, and in
front of the brick Tavern, is a good landing place, for any kind
of a craft.

At the foot of this eddy, commences Brady's Bend.

Around the bend, on the left, a little below the coal scaffold, under a point of rocks, is a good landing place for one
or two large rafts. This eddy is easy to land in, as you have
to pull out of it to get into it.

SUGAR CREEK RAPIDS and BARS. - - - -   2¼   124¼

Keep down the left shore.

GREAT WESTERN IRON WORKS. On the right, below
the mouth of Sugar Creek, is one of the most extensive estab
lishments in Pennsylvania. It was commenced some fifteen
or sixteen years ago, under the management of Philander Ray
mond, Esq., in connection with several wealthy gentlemen of
New York. The lands of the company, which before selection, were carefuly explored by Mr. Raymond, comprise
every material and facility for prosecuting the Iron business
There are rich deposits of ore, bituminous coal, of the finest
quality, lime stone, forests of timber, water power, and suffi
cient land for agricultural purposes. The process of making
the iron is principaly carried on with bituminous coal, and
coke, in the manner practiced in Wales.

The company has now in operation, four furnaces, two of
which are very large; and rising of thirty puddling, and heating furnaces, a rolling-mill, nail factory, foundry, machine
shop, store, ect., and a beautiful busy town containing over
3,000 inhabitants, has sprung up around the works, as if by
the effect of magic, all belonging to, and owned by the com-

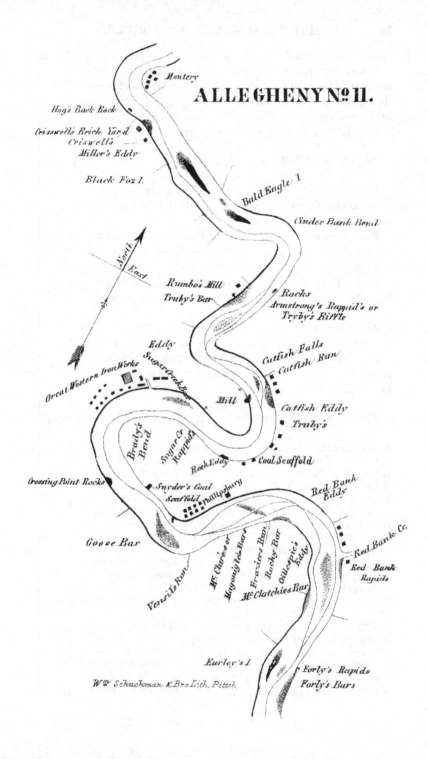

ALLEGHENY Nº 11.

Montery

Hog's Back Rock

Crisswell's Brick Yard
Criswell's
Miller's Eddy

Black Fox I.

Bald Eagle I.

Cinder Bank Bend

North
East

Runbo's Mill
Truby's Bar

Rocks
Armstrong's Rappid's or
Tryby's Riffle

Eddy

Sugar Creek Bar

Great Western Iron Works

Catfish Falls
Catfish Run

Mill

Catfish Eddy
Truby's

Brady's Bend

Sugar Cr. Rappids

Rock Eddy

Coal Scaffold

Crossing Point Rocks

Snyder's Coal
Scaffold

Phillipsbury

Red Bank
Eddy

Goose Bar

Vensile Run

Mc Clarks or
Magonig'es Bar

Brazier's Bar
Rocky Bar
Gillespie's Eddy

Mc Clatchies Bar

Red Bank Cr.

Red Bank
Rapids

Earley's I.

Wᵐ Schuchman & Bro Lith. Pittsb.

Forly's Rapids
Forly's Bars

pany who furnish employment for all of the laborers. Immence quantities of T rail road iron has been manufactured here. The establishment is carried on at an expence of between 1500 and 2,000 dollars ber day.

GOOSE BAR. - - - - - - - - - - -   2¾   127¼

Channel to the left. The main portion of this bar is situated in the short turn, opposite to where the point of the mountain comes down to the river on the left, below Snyder's coal scaffold. The head of the bar extends diagonally upwards, towards, and nearly to the coal scaffold.

To pass this bar systematically, when around to the crossing point rocks, on the right, about half of a mile above the coal scaffold, commence working gradually over to the left. The crossing is very easy, a raft needs but little pulling. The crossing point rocks may be known by a thick grove of hemlocks back of them.

McCLURE'S or MAGONIGLE'S BARS. - - -   1¼   128¾

Channel to the left. In low water, be close to the left shore when opposite a house standing alone about half a mile below the town of Phillipsburg. In good running stages keep down the right shore, till past the bars, then incline out to the left to avoid a rocky bar below the mouth of Frazier's Run. Below the rocky bar, on the right, is Gillespie's Eddy, Redbank Eddy on the left.

The name given to Brady's Bend is derived from one Samuel Brady. the captain of the spies. He was a successful partisan officer against the Indians, in the war of the revolution. There are several traditional reports of the adventures and exploits of this distinguished individual, some of which need confirmation. We give below a portion of his early history, and several incidents that are copied from authentic documents, one of which occured at the Bend, probably not far from these bars. These sketches were written by Mr. M'Cabe, of Indiana, and the facts were principally derived from the brother of Capt. Brady, who lived in Indiana County.

Capt. Samuel Brady was born in Shippinsburg, in Cumberland co., Pa., in 1758, but soon after removed with his father to the West Branch of the Susquehanna, a few miles above Northumberland. Cradled amid the alarms and excitements of a frontier exposed to savage warfare, Brady's military propensities were very early developed. He eagerly sought a post in the revolutionary army; was at the siege of Boston ; a lieutenant at the massacre of Paoli; and in 1779 was ordered to Fort Pitt with the regiment under Gen. Broadhead. A short time previous to this, both his father and his brother had fallen by the hands of Indians; and from that moment Brady took a solemn oath of vengeance against all Indians. And his future life was devoted to the fulfillment of his vow. While Gen. Broadhead held command of Fort Pitt, (1780-81,) Brady was often selected to command small scouting parties sent into the Indian country north and west of the fort, to watch the movements of the savages ; a charge which Brady always fulfilled with his characteristic courage and sagacity

The following Narative is given by Kiskiminetas in the Blairsville Record :

The incursions of the Indians had become so frequent, and their outrages so alarming, that it was thought advisable to retaliate upon them the injuries of war, and carry into the country occupied by them the same system of destructive warfare with which they had visited the settlements. For this purpose an adequate force was provided, under the immediate command of Gen. Broadhead, the command of the advanced guards of which was confined to Capt. Samuel Brady.

The troops proceeded up the Allegheny river, and had arived at the flat of land opposite the mouth of Redbank creek, without encountering an enemy. Brady and his rangers were some distance in front of the main body, as their duty required, when they suddenly discovered a war party of Indians approaching them. Relying on the strength of the main body and its ability to force the Indians to retreat,—and anticipating. as Napoleon did in the battle with the Mamelukes, that when driven back they would return upon the same route they had advanced on, Brady permitted them to proceed without hindrance, and hastened to seize a narrow pass higher up the river, where the rocks, nearly perpendicular, approach the river, and where a few determined men might successfully combat superior numbers. In a short time the Indians encountered the main body under Broadhead, and were driven back. In full and swift retreat they pressed on to gain the pass between the rocks and the river, but it was occupied by their daring and relentless foe, Brady and his rangers, who failed not to pour into their flying columns a most destructive fire.

The Indians on this occsion were broken, routed, and forced to jump into the river. Many were killed on the bank, and many more in the stream. Our aged friend Cornplanter, chief of the Senecas, then a young man, saved himself by swimming, as did several others of the party.

After they had crossed the river, as Brady was standing on the bank wiping his rifle, an Indian, exasperated at the unexpected defeat and disgraceful retreat of his party, and supposing himself now safe from the well-known and abhorred enemy of his race, commenced a species of conversation with him in broken English which we call *blackguarding*— calling Brady and his men cowards, squaws, and the like, and putting himself in such attitudes as he probably thought would be most expressive of his utter contempt of them.

When Brady had cleaned his rifle and loaded it, he sat down by an ash sapling, and taking sight about three feet above the Indian, fired. As the gun cracked the Indian was seen to shrink a little, and then limp off. When the main army arrived, a canoe was manned, and Brady and a few men crossed to where the Indians had been seen. They found blood on the ground, and had followed it but a short distance till the Indian jumped up, struck his breast, and said, "I am a man." It was Brady's wish to take him prisoner without doing him further harm. The Indian continued to repeat, "I am a man." "Yes," said an Irishman who was along, "by J———s, you're a purty boy,"—and before Brady could arrest the blow, sunk his tomahawk in the Indian's brains.

The army moved onward, and after destroying all the Indians' corn, and ravaging the Kenjus flats, returned to Pittsburgh.

The story of Brady killing a party of Indians, near a little run opposite the crossing point rocks, we can find no authority for, except tradition, it may be true nevertheless. The story is as follows :—

Brady having learned that the Indians were in force, some twentyfive or thirty in number, at the above named place, with three or four white men as prisoners, whom they were making preparations to burn alive that evening, appeared in full Indian costume, on the top of the mountain opposite to where the Indians were and near to where the coak-yard now stands, and having the advantage of understanding their language, persuaded them to defer burning the prisoners till the next morning, in order, as he represented to them, that himself and his party, some of which were absent, might be collected and be present on the occasion. The Indians readily consented to the arrangement, and after securing their prisoners for the night, betook themselves to sleep. When all was quiet Brady and his comrades went down to Goose bar and there crossed the river, crawled up to their camp and tomahawked them all while asleep, and rescued the prisoners.

We cannot vouch for the truth of this story, but one thing we can vouch for, if the story is true, Brady was certainly punctual.

RED BANK RAPIDS and McCLATCHIES' BARS.　2½　131¼

Channel to the right or left. In low water, after leaving Red Bank Eddy, work gradually over to the right shore point, opposite the mouth of Red Bank creek, and keep near the right shore around in the curve till down to the next right shore point, then wear out towards the middle to avoid a bar on the right, below the point.

In good running stages, keep down to the left of the long middle Bar, and about five rods from the left shore.

EARLY'S ISLAND and FORLY'S RAPIDS. - -　2¼　133½

Channel to the left. In low water, be quite near the left

shore, while passing the head of the Island, to avoid the little
middle bar, then turn out to the right towards the foot of the
Island, to avoid the large bar that makes out from the left
shore.

DIRECTIONS FOR MAP NO. 12.

DICKSON'S FALLS. - - - - - - - - - - | 2½ | 136

In very low water the channel is near the right shore at the
head of the falls. American Furnace on the left.

NELLY'S CHUTE and BAR. - - - - - - - | 2½ | 138½

Channel to the right. In low water keep near the right shore
while passing the head of the bar.
  The rock in the water near the right point about a mile below, is of no account except in very low running.

MAHONING RAPIDS. - - - - - - - - - | 3¼ | 142¼

In low water, after leaving Gray's Eddy, work gradually over
to the right, so as to be about two-thirds across the river
when opposite the mouth of Mahoning creek, and pass between two little stony bars; the left one is about the middle
of the river. When past the bars, incline to the left while
going down the riffle, to avoid a bar on the right.
  In good running stages keep down the left shore.

  The extract given below is another incident in the life of
Capt. Brady, which transpired in this neighborhood, not far
from the mouth of Mahoning creek, it is copied from the
numbers by Kiskiminetas in the Blairsville Record.

  Brady's success as a partisan had acquired for him its usual results—
approbation with some, and envy with others. Some of his brother officers censured the commandent for affording him such frequent opportuni-
ties for honorable distinction. At length open complaint was made,
accompanied by a request, in the nature of a demand, that others should
be permitted to share with Brady the perils and honors of the service,
abroad from the fort. The general apprised Brady of what had passed,
who readily acquiesced in the propriety of the proposed arrangements ; and
an opportunity was not long wanting for testing its efficiency.
  The Indians made an inroad into the Sewickly settlement. committing
the most barbarious murders, of men, women and children ; stealing such

property as was portable, and destroying all else. The alarm was brought
to Pittsburgh, and a party of soldiers, under the command of the emulous
officers, despatched for the protection of the settlement, and chastisement
of the foe. From this expedition Brady was of course excluded ; but the
restraint was irksome to his feelings.

The day after the detachment had marched, Brady solicited premission
from his commander to take a small party for the purpose of "catching
the Indians ;" but was refused. By dint of importunity, however, he at
length wrung from him a reluctant consent, and the command of *five men;*
to this he added his *pet* Indian, and made hasty preparation.

Instead of moving towards Sewickly, as the first detachment had done,
he crossed the Allegheny at Pittsburgh, and proceeded up the river.—
Conjecturing that the Indians had decended that stream in canoes, till
near the settlement, he was careful to examine the mouths of all creeks
coming into it, praticularly from the southeast. At the mouth of Big
Mahoning, about six miles above Kittanning, the canoes were seen drawn
up to its western bank. He instantly retreated down the river, and waited
for night. As soon as it was dark, he made a raft, and crossed to the
Kittanning side. He then proceeded up to the creek, and found that the
Indians had, in the mean time, crossed the creek, as their canoes were
drwn to its uper northeastern bank.

The country on both sides of Mahoning, at its mouth, is rough and
mountainous ; and the stream, which was then high, very rapid. Several
ineffectual attempts were made to wade it; which they at length succeeded
in doing, three or four miles above the canoes. Next a fire was made,
there clothing dried, and arms inspected ; and the party moved towards
the Indian camp, which was pitched on the seckond bank of the river.—
Brady placed his men at some ditance, on the lower or first bank.

The Iudians had brought from Sewickly a stallion, which they had
fettered and turned to pasture on the lower bank. An Indian, probably
the owner, under the *law of arms,* came frequently down to him, and oc-
casioned the party no little trouble. The horse, too, seemed willing to
keep their company, and it required considerable circumspection to avoid
all intercourse with either. Brady became so provoked that he had a
strong inclination to tomahawk the Indian, but his calmer judgment re-
pudiated the act, as likely to put to hazard a more decisive and important
achievement.

At length the Indians seemed quiet, and the captain determined to pay
them a closer visit. He had got quite near their fires ; his *pet* Indian had
caught him by the hair and gave it a pluck, intimating his advic to retire,
which he would not venture to whisper ; but finding Brady regardless of
it, had crawled off—when the captain, who was scanniug their numbers,
and the position of their guns, observed one throw off his blanket and rise
to his feet. It was altogether impracticable for Brady to move without
being seen. He instantly decided to remain where he was, and risk wha,
might happen. He drew his head slowly beneath the brow of the bank,
Putting his forehead to the earth for concealment. His next sensation
was that of warm water poured into the hollow of his neck, as from the
spout of a teapot, which, trickling down his back over the chilled skin,
produced a felling that even his iron nerves could scarcely master. He
felt quietly for his tomahawk, and had it been about him he probably

would have used it; but he had divested himself even of that when he
prepared to approach the fire, lest by striking against the stones or gravel, it might give alarm. He was compelled, therefore, "nolens volens,"
to submit to this very unpleasant operation, until it should please his war-
riorship to refrain; which ho soon did, and returning to his place wrapped
himself up in his blanket, and composed himself for sleep as if nothing
had happened.

Brady returned to, and posted his men, and in the deepest silence all
awaited the break of day. When it appeared the Indians arose and stood
around the fires; exulting, doubtless, in the scalps they had taken, the
plunder they had acquired, and the injury they had inflicted on their enemies. Precarious joy—short-lived triumph ! The *avenger of blood* was
beside him! At a signal given, seven rifles cracked, and five Indians were
dead ere they fell. Brady's well-known war-cry was heard, his party was
among them, and their guns (mostly empty) were all secured. The remaining Indians instantly fled and disappeared. One was pursued by
the trace of his blood, which he seems to have succeeded in stanching.—
The *pet* Indian then imitated the cry of a young wolf, which was answered
by the wounded man, and the pursuit again renewed. A second time the
wolf-cry was given and answered, and the pursuit continued into a wind-
fall. Here he must have espied his pursuers, for he answered no more.
Brady found his remains there three weeks afterwards, being led to the
place by ravens that were preying on the carcass. The horse was un-
fettered, the plunder gathered, and the party commenced their return to
Pittsburgh, most of them decending in the Indian canoes. Three days
after their return, the first detachment came in. They reported that they
had followed the Indians closely, but that the latter had got into their
canoes and made their escape.

MAHONING ISLANDS. - - - - - - - - | 2¼ | 144½

Channel to the left. While going down the reach above the Islands, keep a little to the right of the middle, to avoid the large
flat bar on the left, and when past the head bar of the first
Island, incline to the left, and run around quite near the left
shore to avoid being drawn upon the bars of the second Island
by the strong current that runs between the Islands. A bar
makes out from about the middle of the second Island, and
reaches nearly half way to the left shore. Coon s rock on
the left point below, about five rods from shore. Barton's
Eddy in the bend on the right.

To the right of the first Island is frequently dry.

PINE CREEK BARS. - - - - - - - - - | 3¼ | 147¾

In low water, make calculations while going down the reach
above, to be a little to the left of the middle of the river when
opposite the mouth of Pine Creek, and pass between the two

ALLEGHENY Nº 12.

Mahoning
Be Gray's Eddy
Mahoning Cr.
Orrville
American Furnace
Rock
Nelley's Bar
Dicksons Falls
Nelly's Chute
Nelly's Bend
Mahoning Isls.
North
East
Orehill Furnace
Coon's Rock
Pine Gr. Bars
Pine Gr.
Pattens Eddy
Hay's Run
Tars I.
Hick's Bar.
Cownshannosk Bars
Cownshannock Cr.
Rocky Shore
Castaway Bar

Wm Schuchman & Bro. Lith. Pittsb.

bars; the one on the left in front of the mouth of the creek, and the long middle bar which is a little to the right of the middle of the river. The deepest water is a little the nearest this bar.

In good running stages, keep down near the right shore, and when down the riffle, cross over to the left.

Pattten's Eddy on the right below the riffle.

TAR'S ISLAND. - - - - - - - - - - -	2	149¾

Channel to the left. Keep near the left shore while passing the head bar of the Island, then turn to the right and run quite near to the foot of the Island, to avoid the Cownshannock bars on the left, above and below the mouth of Cownshannock creek; and from the foot of the Island make a long crossing to the left shore, to avoid Hicks' bar on the right. The deepest water past this bar is within four or five rods of the left shore. When past the bar, cross back to the right again quite near to the rocky shore to prepare for Castaway Bars.

DIRECTIONS FOR MAP NO. 13.

CASTAWAY BAR. - - - - - - - - - -	2¾	152½

Channel to the right. This bar extends from the left shore near the Roman Catholic Church, diagonally upwards about a mile, and nearly across to the rocky shore. The head of the bar is to be seen on map No. 12, the remainder at the commencement of map No. 13. Keep quite near the right shore till past the mouth of Pine Hollow run, then incline a little to the left to pass the little bar below the mouth of the run.

In high water, flat boats and small pieces of lumber after leaving Hicks' bar, can keep down the left shore and go through the separation in the bar, but it should not be done unless for the purpose of landing in Kittanning.

KITTANNING BRIDGE. - - - - - - - ·	1¼	153¾

Channel first or second space from the right shore. Second space is the deepest. After passing the bridge, keep near the right shore till past the bar situated in about the middle of the river in front of the Rolling Works at the lower end of the town. In good running stages, flat boats and the like can go to the left of the bar.

Blue Rock Eddy on the left below the bar, and a little above the town of Manorville.

KITTANNING, the seat of justice for Armstrong county, is a beautiful town, and as beautifully situated on the left bank of the river. The buildings are principally brick. Four streets run parallel with the river, crossed at right angles by eight others. It was laid out in 1804, and incorporated a borough in 1821; population about 3,000. Kittanning was formerly the site of an old Indian town of the same name, and was a prominent point in the north-western boundary of the last great purchase made by the proprietary government in 1768, at Fort Stanwix. The following account of the destruction of the old Indian town of Kittanning, is from the Pennsylvania Gazette of Sep. 23, 1756. copied in part from an original letter of Col. Armstrong to the Governor of Pennsylvania, and is now among the archives of the state at Harrisburg:

Saturday last, (Sept. 1756,) arrived an express from Col Armstrong, of Cumberland county, with advice that he marched from Fort Shirley on the 30th past, with about 300 of our provincial forces, on an expedition against Kittanniag, a town of our Indian enemies on the Ohio, about 45 miles above Fort Duquesne, (Pittsburgh.) On the 3d instant, he joined the advanced party at the Beaver dams, near Frankstown; and on the 7th, in the evening, being within six miles of Kittanning, the scouts discovered a fire in the road, and reported that there were but three, or at most four Indians at it. It was not thought proper to attempt surprising those Indians at that time, lest if one should escape the town might be alarmed ; so Lieut. Hogg with twelve men was left to watch them, with orders not to fall upon them till daybreak, and our forces turned out of the path, to pass by their fire without disturbing them. About three in the morning, having been guided by the whooping of the Indian warriors at a dance in the town, they reached the river, 100 perches below the body of the town, near a corn-field, in which a number of the enemy lodged out of their cabins, as it was a warm night. As soon as day appeard and the town could be seen, the attack began in the corn-field, through which our people charged, killing several of the enemy, and entered the town.—Captain Jacobs,* the chief of the Indians, gave the warwhoop, and defend-

* Supposed to be father to the Capt. Jacobs, who, with Brant, attempted to kill Gen. Scott when a prisoner at Niagara in the war of 1812 but were prevented by the timely interferance of a British Officer.

ed his house bravely through loop-holes in the logs, and the Indians generally refused quarters which were offered them, declaring they were men and would not be prisoners. Col. Armstrong (who had received a wound in his shoulder by a musket ball) ordered their houses to be set on fire over their heads, which was immediately done. When the Indians were told that they would be burned to death if they did not surrender, one of them replied "he did not care, as he could kill four or five before he died," and as the heat approached, some began to sing. Some, however, burst out of their houses, and attempted to reach the river, but were instantly shot down. Capt. Jacobs, in getting out of a window, was shot, as also his squaw, and a lad called the kings son. The Indians had a number of spare arms in their houses, loaded, which went off in quick succession as the fire came to them; and quantities of gunpowder, which had been stored in every house, blew up from time to time, throwing some of their bodies a great hight in the air. A body of the enemy on the opposite side of the river fired on our people, and were seen to cross the river at a distance. as if to surround our men; they collected some Indian horses that were near the town to carry off the wounded, and then retreated, without going back to the corn-field to pick up those killed there at the beginning of the action.

Several of the enemy were killed in the river as they attempted to escape by fording it, and it was computed that in all between 30 and 40 were destroyed. Eleven English prisoners were released and brought away, who informed the colonel, that besides the powder, (of which the Indians boasted they had enough for ten years war with the english,) there was a great quantity of goods burnt, which the French had made them a present of but ten days before, The prisoners also informed, that that very day two batteaux of French Indians were to join Capt. Jacobs, to march and take Fort Shirley; and that 24 warriors had set out before them the preceding evening,—which proved to be the party that kindled the fire the night before—for our people returning found Lieut. Hogg wounded in three places, and learned that he had in the morning attacked the supposed party of four, at the fire-place, according to orders, but found them too numerous for him. He killed three of them, however, at the first fire, and fought them an hour—when, having lost three of his best men, the rest, as he lay wounded, abandoned him and fled, the enemy pursuing: Captain Mercer being wounded in the action, was carried off by his ensign and eleven men, who left the main body, in their return, to take another road. On the whole it is allowed to be the greatest blow the Indians have received since the war began. The conduct of Col. Armstrong in marching so large a body through the enemy's country and coming so close to the town without being discovered, is deservedly admired and applauded—as well as the bravery of both officers and men in the action.

It is proper to observe that the current tradition among the aged men of the town now is, that no one but old Jacobs was burned in the house; that all the other Indians had gone off. Yet it would seem that Col. Armstrong's official report ought to be true. The site of this house was near where Dr, John Gilpin's now stands; and in exacvating his celer, the bones of old Jacobs were dug up.

After the destruction of the Indian town, the location remained unimproved by white people until near the close of the last century. The land e mained in possession of the Armstrong family; and when the establishment of the county was proposed, Dr. Armstrong of Carlisle, a son of the general, made a donation of the site of the town to the county, on condition of receiving one half the proceeds of the sales of lots.

In the winter of 1837–8, a remarkable gorge occurred in the Allegheny river opposite Kittanning. The ice first gorged 1 ½ miles above town, and caused considerable alarm. It broke, however, and passed the town freely,—but again gorged below. The water thus checked, instantly fell back upon the town, and deluged the whole flat quite to the base of the hill.— Many fears were expressed that the whole town would be swept away.— The ferry-boat passed quite up to the high ground,—and all the inhabitants had escaped to the hills. Providentially the gorge borke after about 20 or 30 minutes, and the frightened inhabitants returned with lightened hearts to their homes.

COGSLEY'S ISLAND. - - - - - - - - - -	1¾	155¼

Channel to the left. After passing the bar at the head of the Island incline to the right to avoid the bar on the left, opposite to the foot of the Island. When past the Island, cross over to the righ and keep near the right shore till past Montgomery's Bars, and till down to

CROOKED CREEK ISLANDS. - - - - -	3	158¼

Channel to the right. In low water run around to the right of the middle bar, which lays about even with the head of the second Island. At the foot of the bar, turn short to the left, towards the Island, to avoid being driven upon the bar that extends upwards from the head of Sloan's Island, on the right and when past this bar, incline to the middle of the river and make a long crossing towards the white rocks on the right shore to prepare for Nicholson's Islands and falls.

In good running stages, rafts run directly over the middle bar spoken of, near the head of the second Island.

NICHOLSON'S ISLANDS and FALLS. - - - -	3¼	161¾

Channel to the right. In good running stages, keep a little to the right of the middle while going down the falls. But in low water, after passing the head of the first Island, incline to the left, and keep near the Islands, and when past the bar a little below the foot of the second Island, keep near the middle of the river till past the corn-field bars, one on the left which extends across the mouth of Taylor's Run, the other on the opposite side, near the town of Clinton,

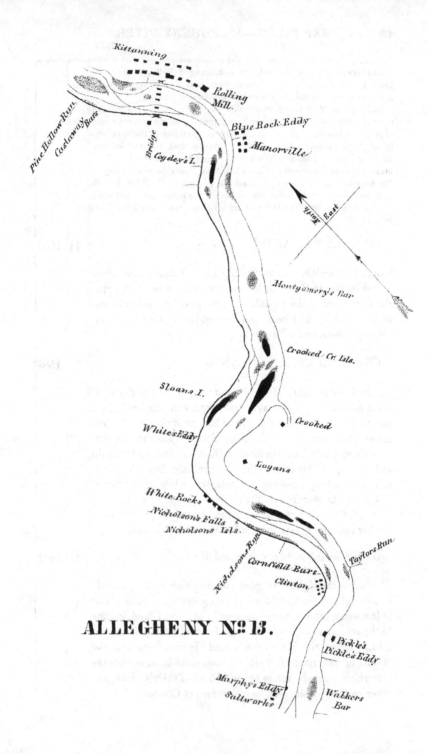

Kittanning

Rolling Mill

Blue Rock Eddy

Manorville

Pine Hollow Run

Castaway Bars

Bridge

Cogley's I.

North East

Montgomery's Bar

Crooked Cr. Isls.

Sloans I.

Crooked

White's Eddy

Logans

White Rocks

Nicholson's Falls

Nicholsons Isls.

Nicholsons Run

Cornfield Bars

Clinton

Taylors Run

ALLEGHENY № 13.

Pickle's

Pickle's Eddy

Murphy's Eddy

Saltworks

Walkers Bar

PICKLES' EDDY on the left. - - - - - -	3	164¾

Is the general landing place on the eve of the third days run
from Warren. After leaving the Eddy, hold well out to
go to the right of Walker's Bar, a short distance below, the
head of the bar extends up to the lower end of the Eddy.

Murphy's Eddy is a mile below, on the right, and immediately below the cinderbank to Hill's Saltworks and about
oposite the foot of Walker's bar. This eddy is very convenient for a few rafts, but it is not as large as Pickles'.

DIRECTIONS FOR MAP NO. 14.

MURPHY'S ISLAND. - - - - - - - -	2	166¾

Channel to the right or left. The rafting channel is to the
right. About midway between the head bar of the Island,
and right shore, is a small lump or bar, rafts can go either
side of it. In very low water Flat boats should go to the left
of the Island, as it is the deepest water and nothing in the
way, except a small rock which lays a little below the middle of, and quite near the Island.

MAD DOG ISLAND. - - - - - - - - -	1½	168¼

Channel to the right. After passing the head bar of the
Island, and while going down the riffle, care should be taken
not to be driven against the right shore. The water presses
hard to the right and is very swift.

AQUEDUCT. - - - - - - - - - - - -	1	169¼

Channel, first or second span from the right shore. Kiskiminitas Creek comes in on the left, below the Aqueduct.

In passing the Rail Road Bridge below the Acqueduct always take the middle space. Look out for this place, it is
well calculated to deceive. The bar on the right shore, a
little below the Aqueduct, turns the main curren out towards
the middle of the river. Many have attempted to go through
the next space to the right, but almost invariably got ship
wrecked on the second pier from the right shore.

FREEPORT. - - - ` - ` - ` - - - ` | 1¼ | 170½

FREEPORT, situated on the right bank, is a flourishing village, and for beauty of location, is second to none on the river. For natural advantages and thoroughfares this place excells. The mouth of Buffalo Creek which comes in at the lower end of the town, is a popular rendezvous for boatmen during the seasons of floods and ice. Freeport Island at the upper part of the village, creates a fine eddy in front of the town, which makes an excellent landing place for rafts of lumber, boats, etc.

The canal from Pittsburgh to Philadelphia, passes directly through here. Four trains of cars on the Allegheny Valley Rail Road also pass by on the opposite side of the river every day. The North Western Rail Road also passes through this place, which is nearly completed, and which is a connecting link, and forms a continuous line of Rail Roads from the Atlantic cities to the far West.

The place contains about twenty-five Stores, Groceries, and Hotels, and nearly as many Mechanic shops, two Foundries etc. Also a large Woolen Factory, and four mills, three of which are propelled by steam, and one by water. It was incorporated a Borough on the 8th of April, 1833; and now contains nearly 2000 inhabitants. There are seven churches in the place; the Methodist Episcopal, Baptist, Presbyterian, Lutheran, Ceceder, Episcopal, and Roman Catholic.

The early history of the country furnishes us with several interesting incidents, one of which relates to the capture of Mrs. Massa Harbison, by the Indians. The sufferings and trials of this distinguished individual while a captive, shows how much humanity can undergo and suffer.

> "When every hope of earthly bliss is gone
> The coward sneaks to death, the brave live on"

If inspired with true fortitude. She was among the first settlers of the conntry, and consequently endured hardships and privations, for a woman, almost beyond human calculation. She is represented as being a woman of strong mind and person, good reputation, and of *tried* courage and fortitude.— She has long since tried the realities, we have every reason to hope, of a better world than this. Several of her children now reside in this place and vicinity, who are second to none in point of respectability.

ALLEGHENY N⁰ 14.

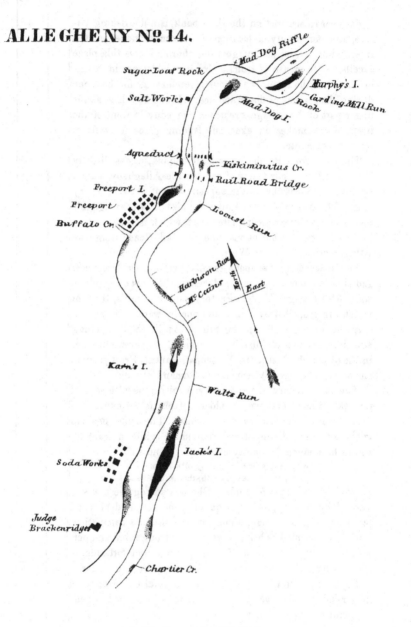

Mad Dog Riffle

Sugar Loaf Rock

Murphy's I.

Salt Works

Carding Mill Run

Mad Dog I.

Rock

Aqueduct

Kiskiminitas Cr.

Rail Road Bridge

Freeport I.

Freeport

Locust Run

Buffalo Cr.

Harbison Run

McCains

North

East

Karn's I.

Walts Run

Jack's I.

Soda Works

Judge
Brackenridge

Chartier Cr.

She was taken captive at her residence, which was situated
about two miles below this place, and on the opposite side of
the rive, a short distance up Harbison's run. After dashing
out the brains of one of her children on the door sill, and
plundered the house, the Indians separated two of which took
her and her remaining two children one an infant in her
arms, and started up the river, and crossed over to Freeport
Island, where she was doomed to witness the murder of her
little boy. She says, in a narative written by herself, "when
I beheld the scalp of my child in the hands of his murder.
ers, with the blood dripping from it, nature gave way and I
fell senseless to the ground with my child under me. The
first thing I remembered after witnessing this spectacle of
woe, was the severe blows I was receiving from the hands of
the savages, though at the time I was unconscious of the injury I was sustaining. After a severe castigation they assisted
me in geting up, and led me into the river, which had the effect to bring me to my senses again."

She remained with them several days, receiving from them
similar treatment, making rapid marches by day, over the
mountains and through the woods, bare foot,—being in a del-
icate situation—carrying her child in her arms, and having it
to care for nights with her hands pinioned. At length she
made her escape while one of the Indians was out reconnoi-
tering, the other having inadvertantly fallen asleep. She was
closely pursued both night and day, and at one time came
very near being retaken. But after several days and nights
wandering to and fro in the woods till worn down with fatigue
and hunger, was at last, through an overruling Providence,
directed to the river opposite to where the fort stood, at the
head of the Six Mile Island. She was taken across to the
fort in a canoe. Her appearance being so materially changed
that her nearest neighbors did not recognize her; she not
having scarcely tasted food for nearly six days.

KARNS' ISLAND. - - - - - - - - - - - | 3 | 173½

Channel to the left. While going down the reach above,
work gradualy over to the left, and when passing the head bar
of the Island, be very near the left shore.

JACK'S ISLAND. - - - - - - - - - -   1½ | 175

Channel to the right. While entering the chute, be a little
nearest the Island, in consequence of a small bar near the
right shore, and a little above the head of the Island, and
when down about to the middle of the Island, incline to the
left, and pass near the foot to avoid a large at bar that makes
out from the right shore.

DIRECTIONS FOR MAP NO. 15.

BULL CREEK ISLAND. - - - - - - - -   3 | 178

Channel to the left. About half a mile below the foot of the
Island, and near the mouth of bull creek, which comes in on
the left, commences the Bull Creek Bars. These bars extend diagonally downward gradually nearing the left shore, for
about three-fourths of a mile, the end of the bars, and the
narrowest, place is exactly even with the lower Salt Works.
After passing the Island keep near the left, and when passing the lower salt works, be very near the left shore. In
very low water be within a few feet of it. When past the
bars, incline out to the middle.

TARENTUM, situated on the right, above the mouth of Bull
Creek, is a well built town. It is 21 miles above Pittsburg,
by the canal, which passes through it. The Locks of the
canal affords an excellent water privilege, and several mills
are propelled, both by water and steam. In the town there
are several Salt works and coal mines. The place contains
the usual supply of Churches, Stores, Shops &c.

PUCKERTY ISLAND. - - - - - - - -   5 | 183

Channel to the left. After passing the bar at the foot of the
Island, keep a little to the left of the middle, till past a large
bar on the left, which extends downward from the mouth of
Poketus Creek
  Logan's Eddy on the left, below the bar.

FOURTEEN MILE ISLAND. - - - - - - -   3¾ | 186¾

Channel to the left. In good running stages, keep the straight
channel and near the left shore, to avoid the large bars that
make out from the Island. In very low water, keep the left,
or crooked channel. (See Chart.) The little bar near the

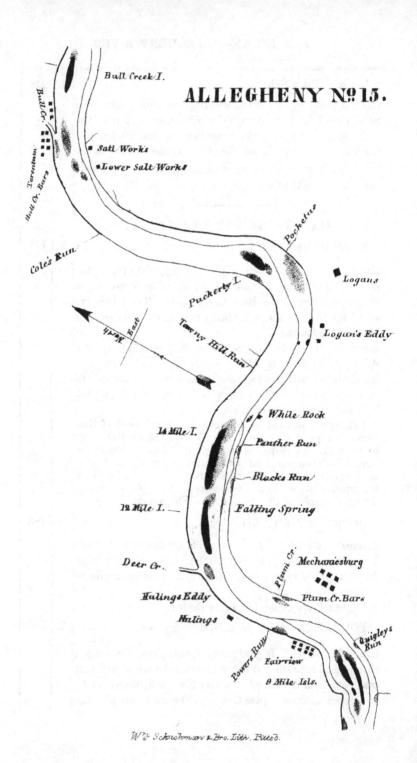

ALLEGHENY № 15.

Bull Creek I.

Bull Cr.

Tarentum

Bull Cr. Bars

Satl Works

Lower Salt Works

Cole's Run

Pocketus

Logans

Puckerty I.

Logan's Eddy

North

East

Tawny Hill Run

White Rock

14 Mile I.

Panther Run

Blacks Run

Falling Spring

12 Mile I.

Deer Cr.

Plum Cr.

Mechanicsburg

Plum Cr. Bars

Hulings Eddy

Hulings

Quigleys Run

Powers Run

Fairview

9 Mile Isls.

Wm. Schuchman & Bro. Lith. Pittsb.

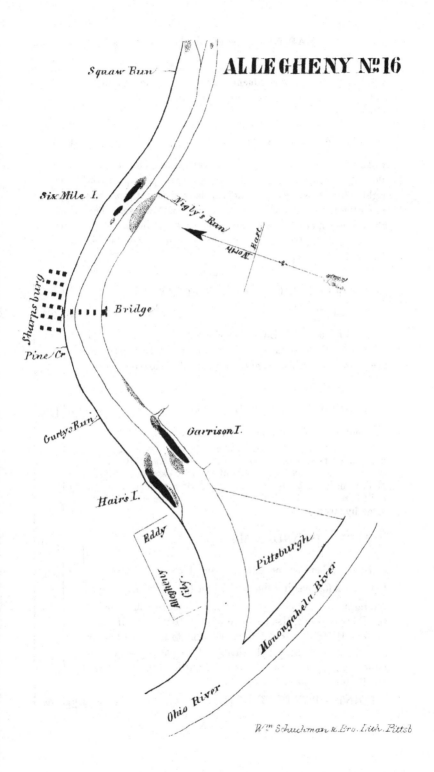

white rock, is of no consequence except in very low running.
Huland's Eddy on the right, below the mouth of Deer
Creek.

NINE MILE ISLAND. - - - - - - - - -	4¾	191½

Channel to the right or left. The best rafting channel is to
the left, although it is not traveled as much, perhaps as the
right. The crossing to the left is made very easy if commenced on the riffle, at Powers' Run, about a mile above. This
channel is not crooked, and much the easiest navigated.

The chart explains the channel to the right of the Island
better than language can.

DIRECTION FOR MAP NO. 16.

SIX MILE ISLAND. - - - - - - - - - -	3¾	195¼

Channel to the left. Enter the chute a little to the right of
the middle, then incline to the right and pass near the foot of
the Island, to avoid a large bar on the left below the mouth
of Nigley's Run.

SHARPSBURG BRIDGE. - - - - - - - -	2	197¼

Channel second space from the right shore.

SHARPSBURG, on the right, is a thriving town. For the
last few years it has grown almost beyond calculation. It
contains several extensive manufactoring establishments, a
Rolling mill, Sash factory, Keel, and Steam boats are also,
built here. It is 5 miles from Pittsburg, by the canal and the
same by river.

HARE'S ISLAND, on the right. - - - - - -	3	200¼

Garrison Island on the left Channel about midway between. After passing the head bar of Hare's Island, hold to
the right, and run close to the foot, in order to either land in
the Eddy below the Island, or to pass the Bridges, In passing the Bridges it is the usual custome to take the first or
second spans from the right shore. After passing the lowermost bridge, incline out so as to be a little to the left of the
middle when opposite the

POINT AT PITTSBURGH. - - - - - - - -	2¾	203

PITTSBURG:

------o------

The seat of Justice for Allegheny County, is situated upon the delta or point of land formed by the junction of the Allegheny and Monongahela rivers, in latitude North, 40° 26′ 25″ and longitude West from Greenwich 79° 59′. It is 300 miles west of Philadelphia, 120 south of Lake Erie, 1,100 by land, and 2,029 by water above New Orleans. The combined waters of the Allegheny and Monongahela, flow on to the Mississippi, under the name of Ohio, or Beautiful River The aborigines and the French, considered the Allegheny and Ohio to be the same stream, and the Monongehela, to be a tributary,. Allegheny being a word in the Deleware language and O-hee-o in the Seneca, both meaning fair water, hence the French term La Belle river, was only a translation of the Indian name. Pittsburg owes its preeminence to the fortunate combination of several natural advantages. It is the center to which all kinds of business for hundreds of miles around gravitates. It is the terminateing poin of the main line of internal improvements, and many extensive thoroughfares; the mart of portions of Virginia and New York, as well as of western Pennsylvania; while the Ohio opens to the enterprise of its citizens, the whole of the Mississippi valley. The exhaustless banks of coal in the neihboring hills, and the excellent mines of iron ore found in great abundance in almost every direction, together with the vast forests of pine timber, on the head waters of the Allegheny, give to this city a preeminence over all others in the west, for manufacturing purposes. To enumerate the various manufacturing establishments of this great work shop, does not fall within the scope of this work. The principal articles of manufacture, are steamboats, both of Iron and wood, steam engines and a great variety of machinery, castings and iron mongery of every description, cutlery, nails, glass, paper, wire, bar-iron, plows, cotton cloths, leather, prints of almost every description, &c., &c. To strangers these manufactories are well worth a visit, especially those of glass, nails, bar and rolled iron. There is much moral power in this city, many men of excellent minds and talent in the learned profession, whose rays of light are shooting forth throughout the world, and many benevolent societies and institutions of learning. The western univeasity of Pennsylvania, commenced its operation as a college, in 1822, and scince that time hundreds have graduated, of whom a great part have devoted themselves to the ministry of the gospel.

Let us go back a hundred years and see what Pittsburg was then. We find it in possession of the French and Indians. They had a Fort here which they called Fort Duquesne, which was a depot of French goods for the savages, and a place of outfits for the Ohio, an important point in the chain of posts, intended to connect Canada with Lousiana. After the British got possession of it, they called it Fort Pitt, in honor of the Earl of Chatham. At this point was considered the key of the west, which commanded the whole Ohio valley, and regulated the trade and intercourse of this immence country, the possession of it became a great object to the contending parties. It was, therefore, strongly garrisoned; and became the common rendezvous of the Indian tribes, traders, soldier, adventurers; and the theatre of many brilliant exploits, skirmishes, and battles in our border warfare. It was near this place where General Braddock was killed and his army defeated, and where Washington gathered his first military laurels. Col. Grant, with his eight hundred Caledonians, was also defeated on the hill just back of the city which bears his name.

The following extracts and communications of the different individuals who figured in those wars and which relate to Braddock's defeat, are copied principley from Craig's History of Pittsburgh. They will give the reader some idea of what Pittsburgh has been the theatre of:

It will be remembered that, at the surrender by Washington, of the fort at Great Meadows, one of the terms of capitulation was that Captain Van Braam and Captain Stobo should be held by the French until the French prisoners taken on the 28th of May should be released.

Captain Stobo was detained in Fort Duquesne for some time before he was sent to Quebec, and on the 29th of July 1754, he wrote the following letter describing the state of affairs here:

"Sir—I wrote you yesterday by an Indian named the Long, or Mono; he will be with you in seven days. This goes by Delaware George. If these discharge their trust, they ought to be well rewarded. The purport of yesterday's letter was to inform you of a report, and I hope false, which greatly alarms the Indians, that the Half King and Monecatooth are killed, their wives and children given to the Catawbas, Cattoways, and Cherokees. I wish a peace may be made up between the Catawbas and the nations here; they are much afraid of them. Many would have joined you ere now, had it not been for that report. There are but 200 men here at this time, 200 more expected in a few days; the rest went off in several detachments, to the amount of 1,000, besides Indians. The Indians have great liberty here; they go out and in when they please, without notice.— If 100 trusty Shawnese, Mingoes, and Delawares were picked out, they might surprise the, fort, lodging themselves under the platform, behind the palisades, by day, and at night secure the guards with their tomahawks. The guard consists of 40 men only, and 5 officers. None lodge in the fort but the guard, except Contrecœur—the rest in bark cabins around the fort. Let the good of the expedition be considered preferable to our safty.— Haste to strike."

The 5th day of July must have been one of great bustle and excitement within the limits of the westward of our City. Within those limits, and near the Point, was then assembled, arounnd and in Fort Duquesne, a number of French and Indians. Intelligence had been brought by their scouts that Braddock, with his formidable and disciplined army was rapidly approaching. The French commandant was, no doubt, greatly distressed and perplexed by the condition of things—his force was comparatively small—fort Duquesne was only a stockade, incapable of resisting, even for an hour, the lightest field-pieces. At this crisis, when it seems the commandant had abandoned all idea of resistance, Captain Beaujeu, a bold and enterprising spirit, well suited to such an emergency, proposed to take a detachment of French and Indians, and meet Braddock on his march.

The consent of the Indians to accompany him was first to be obtained. Capt. Beaujeu is represented to have been a man of great affability of manners, and very popular among the Indians. He went among them, explained his plan, and urged them to go with him. They pronounced the plan a hopeless one, and refused peremptorily to go.

A second time he applied to them—urged them to hold a council on the subjdct; they did so, and again refused to go with him. Still not despairing, Capt. Beaujeu again went among them, used all his arts of persuasion, told them he was determined to go, and asked them whether they would permit him to go alone to meet the enemy. This appeal proved successful. They agreed to accompany him.

This was on the 7th of July, 1755, and they had information that Braddohk was only 18 miles distant. That day and the next was spent in making preparations, and early on the morning of the 9th, the united forces of French and Indians departed, on what seemed an utterly hopeless expedition. Along with Beaujue, were two other captains, Dumas and Lignery, four lieutenants, six ensigns, and two cadets.

"Washington was often heard to say during his lifetime, that the most beautiful spec tacle he had ever beheld was the display of the Brtish troops on this eventful morn ing. Every man was neatly dressed in full uniform; the soldiers were ranged in col umns and marched in exact order; the sun gleamed from their burnished arms ; the river flowed tranquilly on their right, and the deep forest overshadowed them with sol emn grandeur on their left. Officers and men were equally inspirited with cheering hopes and confident anticipations."

At noon they recrossed to the right bank of the river, at a ripple about half a mile below the mouth of Turtle Creek. and ten miles above Fort Duquesne. The ground where the battle first commenced was rolling with ravines on either side, sufficiently deep to con tain, at least, a thousand men, and was covered with a heavy forest, so that the ravines were completely hidden from view. Capt. Orme, an aid of Brddock, who was wounded in the battle, in a letter dated at Fort Cumberland, July, 18th, gives the following partic ulars : "The 9th inst., we passed and repassed the Monongehela by advancing first a party of 300 men, which was immediately followed by another of 200. The general, with the column of artillery, baggage and main body of the army, passed the river the last time about 1 o'clock. As soon as the whole had got on the fort side of the Monongahela, we heard a very heavy and quick fire in our front. We immediately avnanced in order to sustain them, but the detachment of the 200 & 300 men gave way and fell back upon us, which caused such confusion and struck so great a panic among our men, that afterwards no military expedient could be made use of that had any effect on them. The men were so extremely deaf to the exhortation of the general and the officers, that they fired away in the most irregnlar manner all their amunition, and then ran off, leaving to the enemy the artillery, amunition, provisions and baggage ; nor could they be persuaded to stop till they got as far us Gest's plantation, nor there only in part, many of them proceeded as far as Col. Dunbar's party, who lay six miles on this side. The officers were absolutely sacrificed by their unparalleled good behavior, advancing sometimes in bodies and some times separately—hoping by such example to engage the soldiers to follow them; but to no purpose. The general had five horses killed under him, and at last received a wound through the right arm into the lungs, of which he died the 13th inst. Mr. Washington had two horses shot under him, and his clothes shot through in several places; behaving the whole time with the greatest courage and resolution.

By the particular disposition of the French and Indians, it was impossible to judge the number they had that day in the field. Killed—Gen. Braddock, William Shirley, Sec'y Col. Halkett. Wounded—Roger Morris and Robert Orme, aid-de-camps, Sir John St. Clair, Dep. Quarter-master Gen., Matthew Leslie, Asst., Lieut. Col. Gage. Between 6 and 700 officers and soldiers killed and wounded."

Col. Burd, who had obtained his information from Col. Dunbar at Fort Cumberland, also writes : "The battle began at one o'clock of the noon, and continued three hours. The enemy kept behind trees and logs of wood, and cut down our troops as fast as they could advance. The soldiers then insisted much to be allowed to take the trees, which the general denied, and stormed much, calling them cowards; and even went so far as to strike them with his own sword for attempting the trees. Our flankers, and many of our soldiers that did take to the trees were cut off by the fire of our own line, as they fired the ir platoons wherever they saw a smoke or fire. The one half of the army engaged never saw the enemy. Particularly Capt. Waggoner, of the Virginia forces, marched 80 men up to take possession of a hill ; on the top of the hill there lay a large tree about five feet diameter, which Capt. Waggoner intended to make a bulwark of. He marched up to the log with the loss of only three men killed by the enemy, and at the time his sol diers carried their firelocks shonldered. When they came to the log they began to fire upon the enemy. As soon as their fire was discovered by our line, they fired from our line upon him. He was obliged to retreat down the hill, and brought off with him only 30 men out of 80 ; and in this manner were our troops chiefly destroyed. * * The general had with him all his papers, which are entirely fallen into the hands of the ene my, as likewise about £25,000 in cash, All the wagons that were with the general in the action, all the amunition, provision, cattle, &c., two twelve-pounedr cannon, six four pounders, four cohorus and two hortts, with all the shells, &c. The loss of men, as nigh as Col. Dudbar could compute at that time, is 700 killed and wounded, (the one half killed,) and about 40 officers. Col. Dunbar retreated with 1,500 effective men.

Col. Washington wrote to his mother from Fort Cumberland, 18th July, 1755, nine days after the battle : "When we came there we were attacked by a party of French and Indi ans, whose number I am pursunded did not exceed 300 men, while ours consisted of about 1,300 well-armed troops, chiefly regular soldiers. who were struck with such a panic that they behaved with more cowardice than it is possible to conceive. The officers behaved gallantly in order to encourege their men, for which they suffered greatly, there being near 60 killed and wounded—a large proportion of the number we had. The Virginia troops showed a good deal of bravery, and were nearly all killed; for I believe out of three companies that were there, scarcely 30 men are left alive. Capt. Peyrouny and all his officers, down to a corporl, were killed. Capt. Polson had nearly as hard a fate, for only one of his was left. In short, the dastardly behavior of those they call regulars exposed all others that were inclined to do their duty, to almost certain death ; and at last, in despite of all their efforts to the contrary, they ran, as sheep pursued by dogs, and it was immpossible to rally them.

Capts. Ormer and Morris, two of the aids-de-camp, were wounded early in the engagement, which rendered the duty harder upon me, as I was the only person then left to distribute the generel's orders ; which I was scarcely able to do, as I was not half recovered from a violent illness, that had confined me to my bed and wagon for above ten days. I am still in a weak and feble condition, which induces me to halt here two or three days, in the hope of recovering a little strength to enable me to proceed homeward."

And to his brother John he wrtee at the same time · "As I have heard since my arrival at this place, a circumstantial account of my death and dying speech, I take this early opportunity of contradicting the first, and of assuring you that I have not yet composed the latter. But, by the all-powerful dispensations of Providence, I have been protected beyond all human probability or expectation ; for I had four bullets through my coat,* and two horses shot under me, yet escaped unhurt, although death was levelling my companions on every side of me!"

It appears that Washington's estimate of the numbers of the enemy was underrated. Mr. Sparks ascertained that they were about 850, of whom two-thirds were Indians.

Various estimates are given of the force of the French and Indians. The largest estimate is two hundred and fifty French and Canadians, and six hundred and forty Indians. The lowest estimate reduces the number of white men to two hundred and thirty-five, and Indians to six hundred.

The brave and enterprising Beaujeu fell at the first fire, and the victory was achieved under the command of Capt. Dumas.

Again, on the evening of that memorable day—if the statement of Col. James Smith, who had been some time a prisoner in Fort Duquesne, may be relied on—the Point was the scene of savage ferocity aud human suffering.

He says, on the morning of the 9th ——, he observed an unusual bustle in the Fort. The Indians stood in crowds at the great gate, armed and painted. Many barrels of powder, balls, flints, etc., were brought out to them, from which each warrior helped himself to such articles as he required. They were soon joined by a small detachment of French regulars, when the whole party marched off together. He had a full' view of them as they passed, and was confident that they could not exceed four hnndred men. He soon learned that it was detached against Braddock, who was now within a few miles of the Fort; but from their great inferiority of numbers, he regarded their destruction as certain, and looked joyfully to the arrival of Braddock in the evening, as the hour which was to deliver him from the power of the Indians. In the afternoon, however, an Indian runner arrived with far different intelligence. The battle had not yet ended when he left the field; but he announced that the English had been surrounded, and were shot down in heaps by an invisible enemy; that instead of flying at once or rushing upon their concealed, foe, they appeared completely bewildered, huddled together in the centre of the ring, and before sundown there would not be a man of them alive. This intelligence fell like a thunderbolt upon Smith, who now saw himself irretrievably in the power of the savages, and could look forward to nothing but torture or endless captivity. He waited anxiously for further intelligence, still hoping that the fortune of the day might change. But about sunset, he heard at a distance the well known scalp halloo, followed by wild, joyful shrieks, and accompanied by long continued firing. This too surely announced the fate of the day. About dusk, the party returned to the fort, driving before them twelve British regulars, stripped naked, with their faces painted black! an evidence that the unhappy wretches were devoted to death. Next came the Indians, displaying their bloody scalps, of which they had immense numbers, and dressed in the scarlot coats sashes and

---

*When Washington went to the Ohio, in 1770, to explore wild lands near the mouth of the Kenhawa river, he met an aged Indian chief, who told him, through an interpreter, that during the battle of Braddock's field he had singled him out as a conspicuous object, fired his rifle at him many times, and directed his young warriors to do the same ; but none of his balls took effect. He was then persuaded that the young hero was under the special guardianship of the Great Spirit, and ceased firing at him. He had now come a long way to pay homage to the man who was the particular favorite of heaven, and who could never die in battle.

military hats of the officers and soldiers. Behind all came a train of baggage horses, ladened with piles of scalps, canteens, and all the accoutrements of British soldiers. The savages appeared frantic with joy, and when Smith beheld them entering the Fort, dancing, yelling, brandishing their red tomahawks, and waving their scalps in the air, while the great guns of the Fort replied to the incessant discharge of rifles without, he said that it looked as if h—l had given a holiday, and turned loose its inhabitans upon the upper world. The melencholy spectacle was the band of prisoners. They appeared dejected and anxious. Poor fellows! They had but a few months before left London, at the command of their superiors, and we may easily immagine their feelings at the strange and dreadful spectacle around them. The yells of delight and congratulation were scarcely over, when those of vengeance began. The devoted prisoners (British regulars,) were led out from the Fort to the banks of the Allegheny, and to the eternal disgrace of the French commandant, were there burnt to death, with the most awful tortures. Smith stood upon the battlements, and witnessed the shocking spectacle. The prisoner was tied to a stake, with his hands raisen above his head, stripped naked, and surrounded by Indians. They would touch him with red hot Irons, and stick his body full of pine splinters, and set them on fire—drowning the shrieks of the victim in the yells of delight with which they danced around him. His companions in the mean time stood in a group near the stake, and had a foretaste of what was in reserve for each of them. As fast as one prisoner died under his tortures, another filled his place, until the whole perished. All this took place so near the Fort, that every scream of the victims must have rang in the ears of the French commandant!

Gen. Braddock was a brave man, and had enjoyed much experiance in military life; but he was naturally haughty, imperious, and self-complacent disdaining to receive counsel from his subordination, and, what was less excusable in a general, despiseing his enemy. These peculiarities of his personal character were undoubtedly the cause of losing his army, and his own life. While on his march, Col. Croghan, from Pennsylvania, a distinguished frontier-man, with a hundred Indians, offered his services to aid the expedition by scouring the forest in advance of the army and bringing intelligence of the enemy's movements. Washington, with his peculiar modesty and courtesy, advised him to accept their aid; his advice was apparently listened to; but the Indians were treated so coolly that they withdrew in disguet. Braddock not only despised Indians, but all Indian modes of fighting; denouncing the habit of the provincial troops of fighting Indians from behind trees, and insisting upon their coming out upon the open field, "like Englishmen." The provincial troops were no dastards; and could they with their favorite champion, have had their own way, the fortunes of that fatal day would have been changed.

After Braddock fell, the retreating soldiers carried their wounded general for four days, until they reached seven miles beyond Dunbar's Camp, where he expired. He was buried in the center of the road which his advancing army had cut; and to prevent the discovry of the grave, and to save the body from savage dishonor, soldiers, horses and wagons were passed over it. Some of the soldiers so marked the trees near the spot, that those who visited the west many years after could point it out with certainty. It is near a small ru.., a few rods north of the national road, between the 53d and 54th mile from Cumberland, and a little west of the Braddock's run tavern, kept by Mr. R. Shaw. The present national road deviates from Braddock's road near Mr. Shaw's, and crosses Laurel hill by a more southerly route. Before this was located, the old road was the great thoroughfare between the Monongahela settlements and Baltimore. Some twenty years since, while a party of laborers were repairing the old road, and digging away the slope of the hill, they aisinterred some bones, with sundry military trappings, which were at once known by the old settlers to be those of Braddock. One and another took several of the most prominent bones, and the others were re-interred uder the tree on the hill, near the national road. Mr. Stewart of Uniontown, (father of the Hon. Andrew Stewart,) afterwards collected the scattered bones from the indviduals who had taken them, and sent them, it is believed, to Peale's museum in Philadelphia. A plain shingle, marked "Braddock's Grave," nailed to the tree where a part of the bones are reinterred, is the only monument to point out to the traveler the resting-place of the prond and brave but unfortunate Braddock. Thus we see the trutbfulness of the proverb verified, that, "pride goeth before distruction, and a haughty spirit before a fall."

There had long exisied a traddition in the reigon that Braddock was killed by one of his own men, and more recent developments leave little or no doubt of the fact. A recent writer in the National Intelligencer, whose authority is good on such points, says:

"When my father was removing with his family to the west, one of the Fausetts kept a public house to the eastward from, and near where Uniontown now stands, as the county seat of Fayette, Pa. This man's house we lodged in about the 10th of October, 1781, twenty six years and a few months after Braddock's defeat, and there it was made any thing but a secret, that one of the family dealt the death blow to the British general. Thirteen years afterwards I met Thomas Fausett in Fayette Co., then, as he told me, in his 70th year. To him I put the plain question, and received the plain reply, "*I did shoot him !*" He then went on to insist, that, by doing so, he contributed to save what was left of the army. In brief, in my youth I never heard the fact either doubted or blamed, that Fausett shot Braddock.

Hon. Andrew Stewart says he knew, and often conversed with Tom Fausett, who did not hesitate to avow in the presence of his friends that he shot Gen. Braddock, Fausett was a man of gigantic frame, of uncivilized half-savage propensities, and spent most of his life among the mountains as a hermit, living on game which he killed. He would occasionally come into town and get drunk. Sometimes he would repel inquiries into the affair of Braddock's death by putting his fingers to his lips, and uttering a sort of buzzing sound; at other he would burst into tears, and appear greatly agitated by conflicting passions.

In spite of Braddock's silly order that the troops should not protect themselves behind the trees, Joseph Fausett had taken such a position, when Braddock rode up in a psss ion, and struck him down with his sword. Tom Fausett, who was but a short distance from his brother, saw the whole transaction, and immediately drew up his rifle and shot Braddock through the lungs, partly in revenge for the outrage upon his brother; and partly, as he always alleged, to get the general out of the way, and thus save the remainder of the gallant band who had been sacrificed to his obstinancy and want of experience in frontier warfare.

THE IRON CITY COMMERCIAL COLLEGE,

Is an admirably conducted and flourishing institution. It is a college for the business man, and is of immence importance in a large commercial city like Pittsburgh. The fact that the Iron City College has alredy, in the first year of its existance, numbred upwards of four hundred students, most of them from the city, where the parents and friends of the students can have an opportunity of personal acquaintance with its advantages, speaks loudly in praise of the ability, industry and fitness to teach of the gentlemen who compose its faculty. There are at the present time in attendance in various department of the ins itution, upwards of one hundred gentlemen and about one hundred ladies, many of them and especially of the latter, with the design of preparing themselves for the business of teaching. The rooms occupied by the College are finely located at the corner of Fifth and Smithfield streets, directly opposite the Post Office. They are spacious, light and airy, and fittd up in an excellent style for the accommodation of the students. The main room, occupied by the gentlmen as a study room for book keeping, writing mathematics, etc., is sixty feet by forty-three. The ladies' room is forty by twenty feet.— There is also a room devoted to the teaching of drawing, which is thirty-seven by eighteen feet. Instructions are given day and evening. Prof. F. W, Jenkins is the Principal of the Institution. Professor I. I. Hitchcock, author of a new treaties on Book Keeping, teaches the science of account; Mr. John Fleming, author of the "National System of Book Keeping," is the lecturer on the science of accounts and on business, its customs and usages. Alex. Cowley, Esq., Professor of Pennmanship—and a very skilled and competent one, if we may judge from a great variety of specimens executed by him which we have seen, as well as the acknowledged improvement of the pupils he teaches. Dr. Bacon is Professor of Mathematics, Political Economy and commercial Geography. This corps of instructors is certainly a very full and complete one. In all the departments the Principal assists, and of the large number of pupils who have been attending the College, not one but has made commendable progress.

In the Polytechnic department, C. Bartberger, Esq., the talented and well known architect of St. Paul's Cathedral, teaches architectural drawing; E. Morganroth, sculptor, teaches ornamental drawing: S. Loew, Esq., is Professor of Civil Engineering; A. Heddeus., Esq., one of the City Regulators, is teacher of mechanical drawing, and J. L. Koethen, Esq., teacher of Modern Languages. In all its departments, the means of acquiring the desired knowledge are very complete in the Iron City College. In addition to what we have mentioned above, there are lectures from time to time upon educational subjects. James H. Hopkins, Esq., a young and talented member of the Pittsburgh Bar, is the regular lecturer upon Commercial Law.

In conclusion, we can say to those residing at a distance, who may send their sons or their daughters hither to acquire a good practical education, that they will find no better opportunity to do so than at the Iron City Commercial College.

CONCLUSION.

To the reflecting lover of nature in its primeval state, the Allegheny river will always have its peculiar charms. Although associated in the mind with many a scene of blood and strife, human suffering, war and devastation, scalping knife, hair breadth escapes, and all the horrors of savage warfare, the clear and beautiful Allegheny gliding over its polished pebbles, is one of the loveliest streams that ever glistened to the light of the moon.

Having found a home on its peaceful bosom for an eighteen month, during which time we never enjoyed ourselves better, or passed time more pleasantly. We have been treated with every degree of kindness and hospitality by the innabitants, at almost every landing place between Warren and Pittsburgh; and we verily believe that in the same extent of teritory no people exist, who for high christian attainment, hospitality, kindness and disinterested friendship, exceed those who reside on the banks of the Allegheny river.

We wish to impress these facts upon the minds of many of our friends who follow the river in the capacity of lumbermen, that if by any dispensation of providence while following the river, they were deprived of health (which we are all liable to be) and in distress and need friends, they would probably have the opportunity of confirming the above statement.

But a word or two to a certain class, who are not the worst people in the world, naturally, and who in reality are not so bad as they strive to make themselves; and while at home in their own immediate neighborhoods, conduct themselves in quite a respectable manner; but the moment their feet are placed upon a raft of lumber, they seem to be cut loose from every moral restraint, and every principle of morality and virtue, and sink down to the common level with the brute. The mountains from Warren to Pittsburgh, echo and reecho with their loud curses and oaths. The people on shore, both male and female, receive from them all kinds of low vulgar abuse; their property pilfered, their hen-roosts robbed, etc. Drinking, gambling, carousing, and many other demoralizing, body and soul destroyidg practices are pursued by them.

Now then, friends, as you are rationable and reasonable beings, we will address you as such. You undoubtedly have clear conceptions of right and wrong. We now appeal to your sacred honor. Are you satisfied with yourselves? Do you feel as though you were doing right in thus profligating away your precious time, wasting your strength, destroying your intellect, and hastening into an untimely grave? I am satisfied that your better judgment teaches you the contrary is the true doctrine, and that you would all join in one loud response, No! Then why in the name of God in the name of everything that is great and good, persist in such a course, and why not resolve immediately to leave it off. The still small voice that

wakes the dead, in trespasses and sin, whispers, *Leave it off!* *Leave it off!* And whenever you are tempted to go out pilfering from those who, although strangers, are ready and willing to become your friends, robbing their hen-roosts, etc.,—"All tnings whatsoever ye would that men should do unto you, do ye even so unto them," is a divine precept that you would do well to remember and obey.

Intemperance has had its pernicious effect throughout the lumbering community, which no one will attempt to deny. Tell me of an argument to make use of against its evils? If there is another gun left that can be brought to bear against this great Railroad to Ruin, we would like to hear it booming forth its loud peal.

We can think of no words more appropriate than those of John B. Gough, who, it is said, speaks from experience; and who, in his life time, has been heard to say that, he would give his right hand if he could only forget some things. Here you have them:

"What fills the alms-houses and the jails?—What hangs yon trembling wretch upon the gallows? It is drink! And we might call upon the tomb to break forth, 'Ye moldering victims! wipe the grave dust crumbling from your brow, stalk forth in your tattered shrouds and bony whiteness, to testify against the drink! Come, come from the gallows, ye spirit-maddened slayer; give up your bloody knife and stalk forth to testify against it! Crawl from the slimy ooze, ye drowned drunkards, and with suffocation's blue and livid lips, speak out against the drink! Unroll the record of the past, and let the recording angel read out the murder indict-ment written in God's book of remembrance; aye let the past be unfolded and the spirits of victims wailing be borne down upon the night blast! Snap your burning chains; ye denizens of the pit, and come up sheeted in the fire, dripping with the flames of hell, and with your trumpet tongues testify against the damnation of the drink.' "

That there is more truth than poetry in the above language, none will atiempt to deny; and among all that God made upright, and in their nos-trils breathed the breath of life; after being convinced of such horrifying truths, truths of such fearful magnitude, can ever dare to lift the fated cup again. Whoever should, let me say to you that you are rushing de-liriously against the bossy shield of the Omnipotent, and precipitating yourself into the jaws of death. Therefore take warning and beware of desperate steps. Remember you are forming characters for eternity, and there is little enough time for the much there is to do. You have none too many days to live sober, honest, upright and christian-like, begin when you may.

If you have done wrong all is required of you is to repent of the wrong you may have done. Leave it off and try to make restitution as far as is in your power; remember that wherever an evil passion is subdued, a sin heartily abjured and left, there is a holy place. Thenceforth put your trust in God, honor Him with a well ordered life; flee every hurtful lust' bury intemperance face downward, label it on the back *No Resurrection!* and vice and folly, woe and wretchedness, are feared and felt no longer The darkest day will pass away, and sunshine, warm and bland, will again return in all its splendor, and awaken anew the slumbering energies of many a down troden and desparing heart.

TABLE OF DISTANCES,

FOR

ALL THE PRINCIPAL WESTERN NAVIGABLE RIVERS.

ALLEGHENY RIVER,

FROM

WARREN TO PITTSBURGH.

WARREN.		
Reese's Eddy.	2¾	2¾
Scott's Eddy.	3¼	6
Brokenstraw Eddy.	1¼	7¼
Dunn's Eddy.	2	9¼
Robert Thompson's Eddy.	4¼	13½
Tidioute.	8½	22
Hemlock Eddy.	5½	27¾
Tionesta.	9¼	36½
Holiman's Eddy.	3	39¾
Hemlock cr., or Clapp's landing.	4¾	44½
Musk Rat Eddy.	1	45½
Pithole Eddy.	3¼	48¾
Horse Creek Eddy.	5	53
Oil Creek Eddy.	5	58
Franklin Bridge.	7	65
Big Sandy Eddy.	11	76
Big Scrubgrass Creek.	7½	83½
Falling Spring	3	86½
Jacob's Eddy.	2¼	88¾
Craigs Eddy.	3¾	92½
Patterson's Falls.	5¼	97¾
Emlenton.	5	102¾
Stump Creek Eddy.	4	106¾
Miler's Eddy.	8½	115¼
Catfish Falls.	7	122¼
Great Wessern Iron Works.	3½	125¾
Redbank.	5½	131¼
Orrville, Mouth of Mahoning.	11	142¼
Kittanning.	11½	153¾
Pickles' Edddy.	11	164¾
Freeport.	5¾	170½
Tarentum.	7½	178
Logan's Eddy.	6	184
Fairvew.	7½	191½
Sharpsburgh.	5¾	197¼
Point at PITTSBURGH.	5¾	203

MONONGAHELA RIVER,
From Pittsburgh to Brownsville.

Dam No.1 & Birmingham.		1
Braddock's Field.	9	10
Dam No.2 & Braddock's crossing.	1	11
McKeesport and mouth of Yaughogheny.	3	14
Elizabeth.	7	21
Dam No., 3.	2	23
Limetown.	5	28
Monongahela City.	4	32
Webster.	4	36
Columbia.	2	38
Jacksonville.	1	39
Dam No., 4.	1	40
Bell Vernon.	2	42
Cookstown.	3	45
Greenfield.	4	49
Albany	3	52
Dam No., 5.	1½	53½
BROWNSVILNE.	3½	75

UPPER MISSISSIPPI RIVER,
From the Falls of St. Anthony Minesota Territory, to Galena Illinois.

Fort Snelling.		8
St. Paul City.	7	15
Caparia.	4	19
Pig's Eye Settlement.	12	31
Vermillion River.	9	40
St. Douglass & St. Croix River.	1	41
Cannon River, Redwingville.	39	71
Rush River.	3	74
Foot of Lake Pepin.	22	96
Chippeway River.	26	122
Tretts' Landing, Mo. T.	2	124
Waparha Prairie.	12	136
Waziaju and Miniho Rivers,	26	162
Black River.	18	180
Root River.	14	194
Bad Axe River.	23	217
Upper Iowa River.	12	229
Lansingtown.	10	239
Prarie Du Chine, Wis.	20	259
Wisconsin river.	5	264
Cassville.	18	282
Dubuque Io.	30	312
Fever River.	20	332
GALENA.	6	338

OHIO AND MISSISSIPPI RIVERS,
From Pittsburgh to New Orleans.

Middletown, Pa.		11
Economy.	8	19
Fredonia.	6	25
Beavertown.	4½	29½
Georgetown.	14½	44
Liverpool.	4	48

eWllsville, O.	4	52
Steubenville.	19	71
Wellsburgh, Va.	6¾	77¾
Warrenton, O.	7	84½
Martinsburgh.	8	92¾
Wheeling, Va.	1	93¾
Bridgeport, opposite Elizabeth-town and Mountsville.	13	106¾
Lanesville, O.	15	121¾
Sisterville, Va.	26½	148¼
Newport, O.	12	160¼
Marietta & Point Harmrn.	19½	179¾
Vienna, Va.	5¾	185½
Parkersburgh, Va. &, Bellpre O.	9¾	192¼
Blennerhasset's Isl. O.	1½	193¾
Troy.	11¾	205¼
Belleville, Va.	4½	209¾
Letartsville & Isl., O.	29	238¾
Pomroy's Landing.	10	248¾
Point Pleasant.	12	260¾
Gallipolis.	4	264¾
Guyandotte, Va.	40	304¾
Burlington, O.	8	312¾
Hanging Rock.	10	322¾
Greenupsburgh, Va.	6	328¾
Wellsburgh, O.	8	336¾
Portsmouth.	12	348¾
Rockville.	17½	366¼
Vanceebuagh, Va.	2	368¼
Concord.	14	382¼
Lanchester, O.	7½	389¾
Maysville Ky. & Aberdeen O.	12	401¾
Charlestown, Ky.	7	408¾
Ripley, O.	2	410¾
Lavanna, O, & Dover Ky.	2	412¾
Higginsport, O.	5	417¾
Agusta, Ky.	4	421¾
Rockspring Landing.	3½	425¼
Mechanicsburgh.	3½	428¾
Neville, O.	3	431¾
Moscow.	2	433¾
Point Pleasant O & Belmont Ky	4½	438¼
Susaanna, O.	4½	442¾
New Richmond, O.	½	443¼
Columbia.	17	460¼
CINCINNATI.	5	465¼
Newport & Covington, Ky., and Lawrenceburgh, Ia.	22	487¼
Peterburgh, Ky.	1	488¼
Aurora, Ia.	4	492¼
Bellview, K.	6¾	499
Rising Sun, Ia.	3	502
Patriot,	12	514
Warsaw, Ky.	11	525
New York, Ia.	½	525½
Ghent, Ky, & Vevay, Ia.	10	535½
Port William, Ky.	10	545½
Madison, Ia., & Milton, Ky.	10	555
Hanover Landing, Ia.	6	561½
New London,	4	565
Bethlehem,	8	573½
Westport, Ky.	6	579
Charleston Landin. Ia.	12	591½
Utica,	5	596½
Jeffersonville.	6	602½
LOUISVILLE, KY.	1	603½

Shippingport,	2	605½
Portland.	½	606
New Albany, Ia.	1½	607½
Bradenburgh, Ky.	37½	647
Lockport, Ia.	3	648
Northampton.	7	655
Amsterdam,	2½	657½
Leavensworth,	8	665
Stephens Point Ky & Rome Ia	40	705
Cloverport, Ky.	11	716
Hawsville,	14	730
Troy, Ia.	6	736
Kockport.	16	755
Owensborough, Ky.	9	764
Scuffletown,	16	783
Sprinklosburgh, Ia.	3	786
Evansville.	15	801
Hendersonville, Ky.	15	816
Mount Vernon, Ia.	26	843
Shawneetown, Ill,	27½	870½
Golconda.	55	925½
Smithland, Ky.	16½	942
Paducah.	12	954
Fort Massac, Ill.	10	964
Wilkinsonville,	17	981
Caledonia.	9	990
New America.	2½	992½
Trinity.	5½	908
MOUTH OF OHIO.	5½	1003½
Iron Banks, Ky.	20	1023½
Chalk Banks.	4¾	1028¼
Mill's Point.	15¼	1043½
New Madrid, Mo.	44½	1087
Little Prarie.	35	1122½
Nedham's cut off, Ten.	24	1146½
Plumb Point Bars.	30	1176½
Fulton.	14	1190
Randolph.	10	1200
Memphis.	77	1267
St. Fransis River, Ark.	83	1350
Helena.	10	1360
Arkansas River.	128	1488
Bolivar Landing Miss	10	1498
Columbia, Ark.	53	1552
Worthington's Landing Miss.	33	1585
Princeton.	12	1598
Tomkin's Settlement.	36½	1633½
Yazoo River, Miss.	38	1671½
Walnut Hill.	10	1681½
Vicksburgh.	2½	1684
Grand Gulf, Miss.	16	1600
Warrenton.	10	1710
Carthage Landing Ark.	19	1729
Point Pleasant.	11	1740
Bruinsburgh.	10	1750
Rodney.	10	2760

Natchez.	40	1800	Cahokia, Ill.	3½	20
Port Adams, La.	54½	1854½	Vide Pouche. Mo.	4	24
St. Francisville.	67	1921½	Bridgewater.	31	55
Baton Rough.	36	1957½	Herculaneum, Ill. & Har-		
Donaldsonville.	57	2014¼	rison, Mo.	½	55½
Whitehall	10¼	2024¾	Fort Chartres.	16	74½
Cantwell Church.	7	2031¾	Simonton's Warehouse.	15	89½
Bonnet Quatr Church.	24	2055¾	Kaskaskia, Ill,	2	91½
Red Church.	16	2071¾	Bainbridge, Mo, & Ham-		
Arnold's Point.	10½	2082¼	burgh, Ill.	58	149½
New Orleans.	14½	2096¾	Cape Giradeau, Mo	9½	159

MISSISSIPPI RIVER,
From the Mouth Missouri, to Cairo or Mouth
of the Ohio.

| | | | Cape le Croix. | 5½ | 164½ |
| St. Louis, Mo, | 16½ | | Cairo, & Moth of Ohio, | 35½ | 200 |

PITTSBURGH
BUSINESS DIRECTORY.

The remaining pages will show that some of the Pittsburgh Merchants and Business Men are in the field, and thoroughly understand the theory of success in business, not to consist in making shillings by pinching sixpences. We have taken much pains to acquire information, necessary to the justification of ourselves in saying what we do in regard to the reputation of the different business establishments, whose Cards are inserted in this Book, and from what we have witnessed ourselves, and from all the information we can gather from the most reliable sources, we do not hesitate to pronounce them as being worthy of occupying a position in the front rank of the *best houses in the West*. Where they are known these recommendations would be entirely out of place, but are intended as assurances only to those who are less acquainted in the city, and who may be there from a distance for the purpose of doing business, and as such we would say to our Allegheny River friends, not to deal with the first man you meet, but look through the following business cards, and then hunt up the houses; it is but a few minutes walk from the Perry Hotel to either of them, and it is better to deal with those you can place confidence in, than those you know nothing about, either by reputation or otherwise.

We wish to call special attention to the card of the establishment of T. J. Craig & Co. as being one of the best of the kind in the city. They are gentlemen in the worthiest acceptation of the term, and as we sincerely believe, their honor and integrety as business men, justly entitle them to the confidence and patronage of all worthy customers. Those wishing any thing in their line, will find it much to their interest to give them a call.

We could very consistently, and would had we room, use the same language in regard to R. E. Sellers, whose card is on the opposite side of this leaf,; and also to W. S. Haven, W. W. Wilson, A. A. Mason, John H. Mellor, W. P. Marshall & Co., James R. Reed & Co. Hall & Co., Samuel West, Bown & Tetley, A. Lyons, M'Cord & Co., H. Childs & Co., Hall & Spear, Joseph Woodwell, A. Culbertson, Morganstern & Brothers, Wm. Schuchman, who done the lithographing for the map in this book, his work speaks for itself, and Hill & Sons.

Also the Perry Hotel, now kept by John Mish, and the Eagle Hotel, kept by M'Masters, they both keep good houses and are moderate in prices.

We confidently refer all lovers of education to P. Duff's Merchants' College as being the oldest in the city, and second to none in the United States.

We saw some ambrotypes at Wertz's Gallery, 53 Fifth street that are not easily beaten. Whoever does beat them must be up in the morning, and it will be necessary for them to know what to go about when they are up, particularly an ambrotype of Ole Bull, the celebrated violinist, taken by Mr. Wertz, which for depth of tone, free and clear chemical action, beauty of perspective, is not easily surpassed; any one wishing any thing in the Daguerrean or Ambrotype line will do well to call at his rooms, we believe he can please the most fastidious.

CHICKERING & SONS'
PIANO FORTES,

MANUFACTURED BY CHICKERING & SONS, BOSTON;

CONSISTING OF

GRAND SQUARE PIANO FORTES,

AND THEIR LATELY INVENTED

PARLOR GRAND PIANO, FOR SALE ONLY BY

JOHN H. MELLOR,

No. 81 Wood Street, between Diamond Alley and Fourth Street.

JOHN H. MELLOR, the exclusive and only Agent for Pittsburgh and Western Pennsylvania, for the Sale of CHICKERING & SONS' Boston PIANO FORTES, begs to return his most sincere thanks to the citizens of Pittsburgh, Allegheny and vicinity, for their liberal patronage, and he has now the pleasure of informing them that, by the increased facilities afforded in the new and splendid Piano Fort Manufactory, recently erected at an expense of over

TWO HUNDRED THOUSAND DOLLARS,

and employed by Chickering & Sons, exclusively for the manufacture of their own Piano Fortes, they will be enabled to keep a full supply at their agency in Pittsburgh, of all the varieties manufactured by them, from the most splendid Grand, Parlor Grand and Square Piano Fortes, to the plain and low-priced Piano Fortes, all of which will be sold invariably

AT BOSTON PRICES.

By the aid of new machinery, and the valuable improvements introduced into the new manufactory of Chickering & Sons, they will be enabled to produce better Piano Fortes than heretofore, WITHOUT INCREASING THE PRICE. Purchasers may also depend on a complete and large stock of their Piano Fortes being kept at the Warerooms in Pittsburgh of all the styles manufactured by them, thereby affording the western purchaser all the advantages of the Boston Market, without expense of transportation or risk.

A Price List and description of Chickering & Sons' Grand, Parlor Grand and Square Piano Fortes, furnished gratis on application by letter or otherwise.

For the character of the above instruments, the subscriber has the pleasure of referring to about

FIVE HUNDRED FAMILIES IN PITTSBURGH

and vicinity, who have purchased and have in use Piano Fortes from the above manufactory, and also to the following Principals of Seminaries who have Chickering & Sons' Piano Fortes in use, and have given their unqualified testimony of their superiority over all others :

Rev. Charles C. Beatty, Principal of Steubenville Female Seminary. Mrs. S. R. Hanna, Principal of Washington Female Seminary H. R. Wilson. M. D. Principal of the Edgeworth Female Seminary, Sewickley, Pa. Rev. Samuel H. Shepley, Principal of Blairsville Female Seminary, Blairsville, Pa. Rev. Joseph P Tailor, Principal of Kenwood Boy's Academy. New Brighton. St. Xavier Female Seminary, Youngstown, Pa. Prof. S. R. Williams, Louisville Academy for Young Ladies, Louisville, Ky. Miss Sarah Thompson, Principal of Female Seminary, at Xenia. Ohio. Hon Arnold Plumer, and J. S. Myers, Esq. Franklin. Mrs. B. F. Weaver, and Rev. A. M Galbraith, Freeport. Reynolds & Curll, Clarion, Pa Shippen & Black, Shippenville, Pa. J Patton Lyon, Currlsville, Pa.

☞ Old Pianos taken in exchange at their full value in payment.
MELODEONS, ORGAN-HARMONIUMS, GUITARS, PIANO MUSIC, MUSIC AND MUSICAL INSTRUMENTS, OF ALL KINDS—WHOLELALE AND BETAIL.

JOHN H. MELLOR.

Sole Agent for Chickering & Sons for Pittsburgh and Western Pennsylvania, No. 81 Wood Street, between Fourth and Diamond Alley.

IRON CITY STOVE WAREHOUSE.

WM. W. BRADSHAW.

THOS. J. CRAIG.

T. J. CRAIG & CO.

(Successors to J. Barndollar,)

No. 134 Wood Street, south side,

Between Fifth Street and Virgin Alley,

PITTSBURGH, PA.

MANUFACTURERS OF

PLAIN, JAPPANED & PRESSED

TIN, COPPER, BRASS & SHEET IRON WARE,

AND DEALERS IN

Every Description of Foundry Castings, consisting of the best im-
proved COOKING, PARLOR & HEATING

STOVES,

Plain and Fancy Grates and Fronts, Tea Kettles, Hollow Ware, Sad
Irons, and Fenders in every variety. We keep constantly on hand
Coal Scuttles, in Copper, Brass, Tin and Sheet Iron, a No. 1 article,
with a full supply of Goods in the above line, suitable to the wants of
Country Merchants, Housekeepers and others, who will find it to their
advantage to give our Stock and Prices an examination before buying
elsewhere. *Remember the place, No. 134 Wood Street.*

N. B.—Roofing, Spouting and Jobbing Work, promptly attended to.

ENTERPRISE WORKS.

BOWN & TETLEY,

136 Wood Street, 2 doors below Virgin Alley,

PITTSBURGH, PA.

MANUFACTURERS OF

RIFLES, SHOT GUNS, &c.

DEALERS IN EVERY VARIETY OF

FIRE ARMS, &C.

HE ALSO, KEEPS ON HAND A GENERAL VARIETY OF

HARDWARE,

CUTLERY, FISHING TACKLE, PERCUSSION CAPS,

OF EVERY VARIETY;

POWDER, SHOT AND BALLS,

ALSO, AGENTS FOR THE FOLLOWING;

SHARP'S CELEBRATED RIFLES,

VOLCANIC PISTOLS,

Shoots 30 times in a minute.

COLTS' CELEBRATED REVOLVERS,

ALLEN'S

REVOLVERS AND RIFLE PISTOLS,

ELLS' REVOLVERS.

Lumbermen look to your interest, you can buy a first rate Rifle for **$10** Cash, warranted to Shoot Correct, or no sale. Mind the No., 136 Wood Street, 2 doors below Virgin Alley, Sign of the BIG GUN.

DUFF'S MERCHANTS' COLLEGE,

Third Street, Pittsburgh, Pa.

Established in 1840. The only institution of the kind in the State, Incorporated by the Legislature.

Duff's Merchants College.

Nearly **4000** Students have been qualified for business in this establishment, and the reputation of its Students, such that many business men will have no others for accountants. The Principal is the only practical merchant in the country at present, devoting his own practical experience in inducting others into the science of Merchandising, Book-keeping, Penmanship, Commercial Computations, Commercial Law, Political Economy, comprising the leading sciences of the Collegiate Course.

The most elegant and costly Diploma yet engraved in the country, awarded to graduates. For full particulars send for Circular by Mail. Refer to any of our City Merchants.

VIEW OF THE CITY OF PITTSBURGH

D.ͬ M'LANE'S CELEBRATED VERMIFUGE & LIVER PILLS.

HEAD QUARTERS OF

FLEMING BROTHERS,

(SUCCESSORS TO J. KIDD & CO.)

No. 60 Wood Street, Pittsburgh,

NOW SOLE PROPRIETORS OF

DR. M'LANE'S CELEBRATED VERMIFUGE AND LIVER PILLS.

Metalmark Books is a joint imprint of The Pennsylvania State University
Press and the Office of Digital Scholarly Publishing at The Pennsylvania State University Libraries. The facsimile editions published under this
imprint are reproductions of out-of-print, public domain works that hold
a significant place in Pennsylvania's rich literary and cultural past.
Metalmark editions are primarily reproduced from the University Libraries' extensive
Pennsylvania collections and in cooperation with other
state libraries. These volumes are available to the public for viewing online
and can be ordered as print-on-demand paperbacks.

LIBRARY OF CONGRESS CATALOGING-IN-PUBLICATION DATA

Babbitt, E. L., author.
The Allegheny pilot : containing a complete chart of the Allegheny River, from
Warren to Pittsburgh / Edwin L. Babbitt.
pages   cm
Originally published: Freeport, Pa. : E.L. Babbitt, 1855.
Summary: "A travel guide to western Pennsylvania's rivers and navigable
waterways, first published in 1855. Includes detailed maps, notes, and charts.
Documents the original path of the Allegheny and its tributaries, which have since
been changed by the Kinzua Dam and other man-made alterations to
the landscape"--Provided by publisher.
Includes a Pittsburgh business directory.
Includes bibliographical references.
ISBN 978-0-271-06211-2 (pbk. : alk. paper)
1. Pilot guides--Allegheny River (Pa. and N.Y.) 2. Allegheny River (Pa. and
N.Y.)--Navigation. 3. Pittsburgh (Pa.)--Directories. I. Title.
VK995.A55B33 2013
623.89'2297486--dc23
2013023837

Printed in the United States of America
Reprinted by The Pennsylvania State University Press, 2012
University Park, PA 16802-1003